Riding

Practices

A series edited by Margret Grebowicz

Riding

Pardis Mahdavi

DUKE UNIVERSITY PRESS
Durham and London
2025

Printed in the United States of America on acid-free paper ∞

Project Editor: Bird Williams

Designed by A. Mattson Gallagher

Typeset in Untitled Serif and General Sans
by Copperline Book Services

Library of Congress Cataloging-in-Publication Data
Names: Mahdavi, Pardis, [date] author.
Title: Riding / Pardis Mahdavi.
Other titles: Practices.
Description: Durham : Duke University Press, 2025. | Series:
Practices | Includes index.
Identifiers: LCCN 2024035135 (print)
LCCN 2024035136 (ebook)
ISBN 9781478031550 (paperback)
ISBN 9781478028406 (hardcover)
ISBN 9781478060628 (ebook)
Subjects: LCSH: Mahdavi, Pardis, [date] | Horsemen and
horsewomen—United States—Biography. | Iranian Americans—
Southwest, New—Ethnic identity. | Horsemanship—Social
aspects. | Caspian horse—Iran—History. | Iranian diaspora. |
Feminist theory.
Classification: LCC SF284.52. M32 A3 2025 (print)
LCC SF284.52. M 32 (ebook)
DDC 798.092—dc23/eng/20241217
LC record available at https://lccn.loc.gov/2024035135
LC ebook record available at https://lccn.loc.gov/2024035136

Cover art: Cover text handwritten by Pardis Mahdavi.

For Tara

CONTENTS

ACKNOWLEDGMENTS

A book like this is as painful to write as it is liberating, and I am most grateful to all the people who held space for me and held me in their spaces as I engaged this project. Margaret Grebowicz and Christopher Schaberg found this story inside me and gave me the courage to write it. It is nothing short of an honor to be in the Practices book series. To the team at Duke University Press—especially my editor, Elizabeth Ault—I can't express my gratitude in words. This has been the most nourishing publishing team I have ever encountered.

There is no developmental editor, word goddess, or writer who compares to Victoria Loustalot. Without her guidance this book would be saved on a distant hard drive in my computer and never see the light of day. I am grateful to Victoria and to my agent, Jess Regel, who give me the confidence to keep writing and who remind me the lessons from falling. My coaches Dick Nodell and Toby Quinn keep me falling and rising up.

My dear friends Yasmin Michael, Riva Kantowitz, Traci Moser, Scott Brooks, Erin Runions, Shar Najafi-Piper, Brandon Lee, and Maggie Angle provided love and support at every turn of these pages. My fellow horsewomen Kimber McKay and Val Thomas, all the ladies at Harmony Stables in Missoula and Rancho Paradiso in Scottsdale, and all the women I rode with in Iran give me faith, fortitude, and hope and help me laugh through my falls. My cowboy always brings a smile to my face.

To my family, most notably my three beautiful children, Tara, Shayan, and Raami, I will always be grateful for your patience when I took time away from you to write because I couldn't keep the words inside me any longer. My parents, Feresheth and Mahmood, and my brothers, Paymohn and Paasha, are always a never-ending well of support, and I will be grateful for them forever.

CLICK. CLACK. CRACKLE. BOOM. The grass beneath my bare feet trembled, and an earth-shaking ba-boom, ba-boom reverberated through my body. I whipped my head around, and my headscarf fell to the ground. What was that? Where was it coming from? My heart skipped several beats, and I wondered—as I did many days living in Iran—if I was in danger.

I had come to my ancestral homeland under the guise of studying the emerging feminist movement in Iran. But some part of me always knew that I'd really come in search of answers about myself and where I belonged in this world. Having grown up in the United States after my parents fled a home country in the throes of revolution, Iran, in my imagination, incited a mix of fear and fantasy. The images I saw on television as an elementary school child were of burning American flags, American hostages taken, and wailing women cloaked from head to toe in black. This was contrasted with the crackling voices of my aunts, cousins, and friends back in Iran during our weekly

phone calls. They told a story of a country with a rich history, a people with strength coursing through our veins, and a youth movement on the rise. When I could no longer stand to only dream about Iran, to fantasize about returning to an imagined homeland where I would finally fit in, finally make sense, finally belong, I decided it was time to go.

I arrived in Tehran in 2000, a fresh-faced twenty-one-year-old, and it took less than a week for me to fall completely in love with the country. I met new relatives, friends of the family, and people from my parents' past. Everyone was eager to show me the "real Iran," thrilled by my insatiable curiosity. And every night I followed my cousins and new friends into a wild underground scene of parties and politics. There, I blended in among throngs of my peers who were living life to an extreme I hadn't experienced growing up in the United States.

This was a side of being Iranian that my family had kept from me. Frozen in the moment of their emigration, my parents, like many others in the diaspora, had raised their children to follow a version of the culture that didn't really exist in the homeland. They'd convinced me that good Iranian girls didn't date, except in an arranged fashion. My grandmother had burned it into my brain that my sole goal ought to be finding a husband, and many in the Iranian-American diaspora told me that being an Iranian feminist was a contradiction in terms.

They were wrong.

Despite, or rather because of, the relentless command of an older generation of conservatives who had taken power during the revolution, the young women I met in Tehran were in charge of their own sexualities; dating, mating, and sleeping with numerous men. These women were leading what they called a sexual revolution, or an *enqelab-i-jensi* in Persian. They talked constantly about their bodies, the resistance they embodied, and the desires they navigated and embraced. Unable to negotiate true citizenship with the state, they negotiated in the bedroom instead. They would take down the regime protesting not in the town square but from the most intimate spaces of their lives.

The Islamist regime that came to power during the Islamic Revolution of 1979 cast a dark shadow of austerity over the country. In public, Iranians were mandated to wear Islamic dress and to refrain from activities such as listening to pop, rap, or heavy metal, dancing, drinking, or fraternizing with the opposite sex outside of marriage. I remember driving by a billboard with an enlarged photograph of Ayatollah Khomeini, the former supreme leader of Iran and the architect of the Iranian revolution. Khomeini was speaking a decree: "The Islamic Revolution was not about fun; there is no fun to be had in the Islamic Republic of Iran." I watched under the light of a full moon as young people spray-painted over the quote while blasting Persian rap and taking turns gulping swigs of what I could only assume was illegally procured or home-brewed alcohol from a blazing silver flask.

Young Tehranis led me into darkened, emboldened corners of the city, and I was both thrilled and terrified to follow. We attended underground, illegal dance classes, raves in the mountains, house parties that shook the walls, and sensual poetry readings in abandoned warehouses. There were also sex parties, where it wasn't uncommon for a hat filled with everyone's keys to be passed around to determine who should hook up with whom.

But Iran's sexual revolution wasn't just about sex; it was sex *and* politics. The mullahs had assured their rise to power by promising the restoration of a certain moral order they claimed had been lost under the shah. They vowed to stop the "Westoxication" that had spread through Iran during much of the twentieth century, and they did so by shrouding the country in a false fabric of morality, a new "dark ages." Young people recognized that this fabric had to be attacked by challenging the moral order. They nicknamed the morality police "the dark patrol" and called themselves "the dawn patrol." A new revolution was brewing, a movement that brought hope to so many people my age struggling with feelings of hopelessness.

In public—with a single strand of hair peeking out from their veils—they were slowly and as safely as possible questioning the regime's legitimacy. But behind closed doors they were quickly and not nearly so safely carving out the necessary spaces to explore, debate, love, breathe. For enhanced privacy, the young people often turned to the cover of the mountains. There, they engaged in intimate acts punishable by death.

This is what had led my date and me to the hills of Kordan, a suburb of Tehran covered in grassy hills and jagged mountains that kissed the cloudless blue sky. Kordan was a haven for Iranians of all ages. My parents' and grandparents' generations enjoyed the open spaces where they could see the sky and plant orchards to grow their favorite fruits. Elderly couples often sat in the shade of their own mulberry or barberry trees, reading a book and licking their fingers after munching on the berries with their delicious nectar. For my generation, Kordan provided a desperately needed escape from the watchful eyes of the crowded city of Tehran. Overgrown trees and bushes on the zigzagging trails up the mountains provided cover for canoodling lovers. Here young people felt more free to gather, dance, discuss political activities, and take in the quiet of nature.

Ali, an aspiring journalist, drove the twisting and stomach-turning roads through the hills until we arrived at a clearing at the foot of Mount Damavand. But before he had a chance to unfurl our fibrous woven blanket thick as carpet, the earth began to shake, and we heard a loud rhythm of pounding beats coming up the trail behind us. *Ba-boom. Ba-boom.* I was terrified. The dark shadow of danger made its way to me.

What was happening? The pounding grew louder, closer, and then I realized—we were hearing hoofbeats. Horses. When they finally came into view, they were magnificent, bold, certain. And riding atop them were women of equal magnificence and bold certainty. The riders opened their mouths and let out a high-pitched trilling.

Hiiii-liiiii-liiii-liii-li. Hiiii-liiii-liiii-li.

I had only ever heard women make this sound at weddings and parties to signal budding romance. Here in the lush plains that grew in the shadow of one of Iran's highest peaks, it seemed both out of place and entirely at home.

I was entranced. They were a group of ten, all riding barefoot, bareback, and bit-free, their hair streaming in the wind behind them. The women were dressed in bright red, pink, and orange; some of them, riding hands-free, held weapons. The leader among them had a bow and arrow pulled taut. The two women who flanked her carried spears. But when the leader met my gaze, she smiled and lowered her weapon, clucking her tongue to signal the others to do the same.

"*Iiist.*" She kicked her legs forward and sat deep into the groove of her black-and-brown horse, bringing him to a halt. The remaining women and horses followed.

They towered over Ali and me. I looked up at their faces, squinting to make out their expressions as the rays of sunshine formed haloes around them. Horses in every shade of black, brown, tan, and white blended perfectly into the chiseled sandstone bluffs that formed the base of the mountain. Some were tall and thin, others stockier with long, shaggy manes and tails. As they grew impatient, eager to be in motion again, they shook their heads and pounded the earth with their hooves.

Feeling ricocheted between horses and riders. Several of the women made clucking sounds to indicate to the trio at the head of the group that they, too, were ready to continue moving. The leader whipped her head to the left, causing the cascade of her long brown curls to fall across her horse's neck. The horse reared up on its hind legs, and the woman flashed a brilliant smile, revealing a dimple. Something inside me stirred when I locked eyes with her horse. He cycled his perfectly muscular two front legs in midair and then set them gently back on the ground. His rider let out a loud laugh that reverberated across the mountains and down my spine.

"Sorry to interrupt young love," she said, almost mockingly. She raised her perfectly arched eyebrows, and I cocked my head. An overwhelming wave of familiarity rushed through me as she spoke, but I couldn't place why or how.

I opened my mouth but found no words. Before I could gather my thoughts, the leader kicked her legs and clucked her tongue to turn not only her horse but all ten horses in the herd. As the drumlike hoofbeats filled the air once more, she turned to catch my eye one last time and winked. Her horse let out a proud neigh and galloped on.

I was quiet the entire drive home. Ali and I hadn't made out after all. Instead, I had watched the women ride off toward the hills, marveling at how their bodies moved in perfect unison with the horses, an almost choreographed dance of hips swishing in tune and time with the rippling muscles of their equines. All I could think of was finding a way to join them. At the age of twenty-two, I had never ridden a horse, but something inside me had shifted, and I understood riding was my destiny.

Later that day, I scoured the books and albums in my aunt's apartment in Tehran. I was searching for clues as to why the woman and horse I had locked souls with looked so familiar. My aunt came home to find me tearing through her library. She took my hand and gently led me to the kitchen, promising to help me find what I was looking for after we filled our bellies. At dinner, I told her the story of the women riders. She listened intently, and a Cheshire cat–like grin spread across her face.

"They sound like Persian warrior women," she said.

My whole body softened at her words. *Persian warrior women*. It had been the story of Gordafarid, the Persian warrior princess, that had first inspired me to learn about my ancestral home as a child, a homeland thousands of miles away that for so long had only existed in my fairy tales.

I was born into a heightened sense of danger. My parents had fled Iran during the Islamic Revolution of 1978. My mother, eight months pregnant with me, boarded what would be the last direct flight from Tehran to the United States for the next forty years. We landed in Minneapolis and began a new life, one my parents hoped would be temporary.

They never even fully unpacked in our Minnesota home by the lake. Farsi remained the only language spoken in our house, which was decorated like a Persian palace from a fairy tale. Time passed. I grew old enough to enter school, where I learned English and reading and math and carried a lunchbox packed with heavily scented Persian food—never mind the snickers and eyerolls from my mostly white Anglo-Saxon Protestant classmates.

The images of Iran on the television contrasted sharply with stories my grandmother and father told me about Persia. With

Iran and America at constant war, what of me, a person who was both countries in one body?

At night, after I finished puzzling through my homework, my father would read to my brother and me from the Persian epic the *Shahnameh*, or "Book of Kings." It was not just a family favorite in the Mahdavi household but a national treasure. Part history, part legend, part mythology, the *Shahnameh* is one of the longest epics ever to be written. The Persian poet Ferdowsi penned the more than 50,000 two-line verses between 977 CE and 1010 CE. The epic focuses on the rise of the Persian Empire and the story of how greater Iran took shape. It is also about bravery, family, culture, and love. And while most of the stories, as the name suggests, are about kings and heroes, my grandmother, and later my daughter, would always point out that the poem should have been called *Shahbanonameh* or "Book of Queens." The female characters, from the queens to the princesses to the brave warrior Gordafarid, were the linchpin to every story Ferdowsi told. The women and the horses.

The epic begins in what Baba called the "Mythical Age." Ferdowsi started with the story of the creation of the world as believed by the Sasanians, the first people to explore and conquer, all on horseback. Save for the horses, this was my *least* favorite part. Two thirds of the epic focused on what was called the "Heroic Age." And while most people fixated on the tales of the kings and conquerors like Alexander the Great, Manuchehr, the legendary Sasanian leader, and Rostam, the great Iranian *pahlevan* (warrior prince), my favorite stories were the ones about women like Tahmineh, the cunning princess who was Rostam's lover and who gave birth to their son in secret. I loved the power of Rudabe and Sudabe, women who inspired the great kings like Zal and Siyavash to lead armies of men and horses into lands unknown. But by far my very favorite was the great warrior princess, Gordafarid. The first time my father read me the story of Gordafarid, I almost cried with joy. Here was a woman I could relate to. Here was a story of real bravery. And it wasn't until much later in my life that I would look back at the six-year-old me, my heart aching for a little girl who related to warriors because she lived in a state of heightened danger, always worried what would come next, who would threaten her, when she would have to leave.

After dinner with my aunt, I went to bed and dreamed of Gordafarid, only now she had the face of the woman rider I had met that day in the hills. Like the Persian paintings that filled the hallways of my childhood home in Minneapolis, scenes of epic battles danced through my dream. But while those Qajar paintings only ever depicted men on horseback (women were shown cooking, dancing, or entertaining men), I dreamed of women wielding swords, bow and arrows, and spears, warriors facing their enemies head on. I didn't know it then, but those women fought with the same fear-induced adrenaline that they harnessed as power and that quietly ate away at them; the same fear that was propelling me forward to fight for belonging and success in my personal and professional lives and also slowly wearing me down in both.

I woke up the next morning determined to ride. I knew I had to learn to ride in my ancestral homeland, on horses that belonged to our native lands. But this would not be easy. Under the Islamic Republic of Iran in the early 2000s, horseback riding for women, particularly unmarried women, was controversial. The hard-line clerics believed that equestrian sports could damage hymens, thereby rendering women ineligible for marriage. Others believed that even married women should not be seen straddling a large animal, for such a sight could ignite the fires of lust in nearby men. I would have to tread carefully to avoid being harassed or targeted by the watchful morality police, who would be happy to have a reason to arrest an Iranian-American woman studying sexual politics in Iran. The danger seduced me.

Luckily, a group of feminists I had been studying in the Iranian underground had a contact for me: a woman named Reyhan who was known for her horsewomanship and organizing prowess. Reyhan trained women to ride in secret as a revolutionary act. She lived and worked in Kordan, the same suburb that hosted hungry lovers and provided refuge to city dwellers growing tired of the constant mayhem of the capital. I made my way to Reyhan's barn the very next day.

A group of women was gathered under an olive tree. They were cleaning and polishing saddles and weaving ropes that I would later learn doubled as reins. None of them wore head-scarves or the Islamically mandated outerwear of long, drape-like coats called *monteaus*. Like the male jockeys I had seen the few times I had attended horse races in the United States, these women wore tight pants called jodhpurs, boots, and T-shirts or tank tops.

One of the taller women, who had a brownish-red pixie cut, came toward me. "I'm Laleh," she said, kissing me on both cheeks. "You must be the American." I stiffened. I hated this reference. I had come to Iran in search of belonging, a way to make sense of who I was and where I came from. But my accent and manners gave me away. Too Iranian in America, too American in Iran.

Laleh introduced me to the three other women gathered in the shade of the branches. My eyes lingered on their faces as I searched for signs of the woman from the other day. I wondered if I'd be able to muster the courage to ask these women if they knew her.

"Come, let's introduce you to Reyhan," Laleh said. She took my hand and guided me toward a small mud house with an even smaller doorway. The cracking walls had been painted a cheerful yellow, and the doorway was framed with turquoise and yellow tiles. I kicked off my shoes and bent my head to follow Laleh inside. The house was comparatively cooler than the scorching summer heat, the cool floor tiles bringing down our body temperatures. The smell of grass mixed with hay, dirt, and horsehair filled my nostrils. I would come to associate this somewhat startling smell with comfort and happiness, the heartbeat of the horses immediately lowering my own.

But Reyhan was nowhere to be found in the house. Laleh offered to take me back to the paddocks and introduce me to some of the horses instead. Butterflies danced inside me. I would finally be close enough to these magnificent creatures to touch them, to inhale them.

"Are you nervous?" Laleh asked. Her emerald-green eyes flickered mischievously.

"I'm excited. I can't wait to get on one." That heady mixture of fear-induced adrenaline and passion coursed through my veins.

Laleh nodded and ran her long, delicate fingers through her cropped hair. "It's even better than you think." She smiled.

As we walked into a grassy area framed by splintering wooden fences, five horses began to wander toward us. They drifted slowly, their heads swaying to the rhythm of their own feet. As they drew closer my eyes floated up to lock with theirs, fixated on their long, silky eyelashes. I stepped back instinctively, suddenly acutely aware of our size difference.

"Don't be afraid. They are gentle giants," Laleh assured me.

"It's just . . . I'm just realizing that they . . . kind of scare the shit out of me," I replied as three horses encircled me.

"Well, the only way is to face your fear."

"Face it or harness it?" I raised my eyebrows.

"You can't exactly harness fear. You can learn to recognize it, to use it, like you do with rage. But either way you must face it. Now, up you go." Laleh looped the red-and-white woven ropes in her hands expertly around the head of a chestnut-colored horse with a black mane. The horse lowered its head with care and bowed its front legs to make her job easier. She gently fingered the mane out of the way of her work, then rubbed the horse between its ears. After securing the reins, Laleh knelt on one knee between the horse and me. She looked at me expectantly.

My eyes widened.

"Sorry, am I supposed to just sit on her back like that?" I asked nervously.

"First, it's a 'he,' and his name is Jahangir. We call him Jahan."

I smiled. His name meant "the world."

"And second, if you can't or don't want to ride him without a saddle—like a real woman—I'll go fetch you something." Laleh stood, towering over me once again, and walked back to the yellow mud house. I watched her walk away and then whipped my head back to Jahan, realizing in that moment that we were alone and I was way out of my league. What if the horse ran away? What if he tried to run me over? But Jahan just stood there calmly licking his lips and bobbing his head as he looked at me expectantly. I hesitantly touched his nose, causing him to lower his head. I rubbed between his ears as I had watched Laleh do moments earlier. As I did so, Jahan's entire body relaxed, and I realized that mine had as well. Just then, my new friend returned with dust-coated blankets and a scarf. Jahan stiffened at the sight of what she carried. He jerked his head up toward the sky. Unaccustomed to horse movements, I startled, lost my footing on the ground, and fell to my hands and knees. I stood quickly, dusting my body—and ego—off. Before I had the chance to ponder whether there would also be a saddle, Laleh had fastened the blankets atop Jahan's back, divided like butterfly wings by the scarf she tied around his belly. He shook his mane, as if to roll his eyes at me.

"No more excuses, up you go." Laleh knelt beside me again, and this time I stepped gingerly on her upper quadriceps, and my belly flopped onto Jahan's back clumsily. Laleh clutched her midsection as her laugh echoed across the farm. Before long, two other women were making their way toward us.

I scrambled as quickly as I could, bruised ribs and ego be damned, and flung my left leg over Jahan's back to come to a straddling sit between the fabric. I gripped the reins tightly, ready to hold on and gallop away into the sunset.

But Jahan stood motionless, chewing lazily on some weeds. Now there were three women laughing at me. My face flushed.

"So, you mounted the American, I see." One of the women chuckled. She looked older than the others, perhaps in her mid-thirties. Her tanned face and chapped lips matched the color of her hair. Her black eyes and eyebrows stood out against the beige canvas of her skin.

"I'm Reyhan," she said. She walked up to Jahan and raised her hand ever so slightly. He obediently lowered his head and front legs, catapulting me forward. As my face landed in his tangled black mane, I couldn't help but laugh at myself. I used my hands to push myself back up to a seat as he rose. My horse's sense of humor was contagious.

"It's . . . ah . . . I'm Pardis." I cleared my throat. "It's nice to meet you."

"I've heard a lot about you," Reyhan replied. She wandered over to a white horse I hadn't noticed. She made the slightest kissing sound with her lips, and the horse walked calmly over to her and bowed. She mounted him effortlessly and then smiled. "You're the sex doctor."

Everyone laughed again.

"*Studying* sex as politics," I corrected her, as gently as I could. I was embarrassed and knew my defenses were rising. But even just sitting on a horse had brought me an enormous sense of calm, one that I wanted to bottle up and store for all the times of uncertainty that raged inside my divided self. That unending quest for conscious self-actualization had led me to my ancestral homeland in search of answers and reassurance.

"So, you're a feminist then?" Laleh asked. I was grateful to be sitting on a horse so I wouldn't have to look up at her. She squinted at me, lifting her left hand to form a canopy over her face for shade.

"It doesn't matter what or who she is," Reyhan interjected. "Right now, she is a rider and nothing more." Reyhan clucked her tongue, and the white horse began an elegant prance-like jog around the arena. He tossed his mane triumphantly as he carried his rider proudly around the arena. In that moment I was torn between wanting to be the horse and wanting to be the rider. I shook my head and then tried to make the same clucking noise with my tongue, but Jahan remained rooted to the ground.

"You have to squeeze your legs when you cluck!" Reyhan called out from the other side of the arena.

My heart was pounding against my rib cage. I did not want to embarrass myself. Did not want to fall. Did not want to fail. Fear threatened to undo me, but then I felt Jahan inhale calmly, expanding his rib cage between my legs, and my blood pressure dropped.

I squeezed with the full force of my underdeveloped thigh muscles. Jahan reluctantly began walking slowly toward the outer edge of the arena. As he lunged forward, my heart leaped and a lightness came over me. I knew I didn't look anything like Reyhan in her marvelous elegance trotting perfectly around the arena, but even this walking slowly, clumsily seated amid scarf-spliced pillows, was exhilarating.

"Nice walk!" Laleh called, interrupting my reverie. She had her arm looped around the waist of the other young woman, whose name I would later learn was Vida, and they were laughing again.

My heart skipped as I looked from Reyhan to Laleh and Vida.

Reyhan's horse picked up speed from a canter to a gallop. I watched as she dropped the reins and leaned back ever so slightly to allow her hips to fuse with her horse's body. She closed her eyes and turned her palms up to the sky, the picture of surrendering to a feeling of ecstasy. She did a few turns around the arena as Laleh, Vida, and I stared. Something inside me stirred—the joy of surrender, I wondered?

"Fly, Reyhan, fly," Laleh called.

Reyhan opened her eyes, leaned forward to grab a fistful of the horse's mane, and then winked at me before disappearing into the trees. I dug my heels into Jahan's sides, determined to follow. But Jahan only picked up the slightest bit of speed, moving from the walk to a slow, jostling trot. I wondered if I'd be bounced off his back. I gripped the reins tighter and squeezed harder. But the death grip of my legs was the signal for speed, I quickly learned. Jahan was trotting faster and faster, and my heart leaped into my throat. I closed my eyes—an instinct that I would learn to fight—and then forced myself to open them. Suddenly, there was Laleh. She had jumped in front of us.

"Ist!" she said, holding up her hand. Jahan stopped in an instant.

"You can't leave the arena until you can ride," Vida tsked. Laleh shook her head and started stroking Jahan's face to calm him.

"I can ride," I said defiantly. I knew it was dangerous, but that only increased my hunger. I needed to fly.

"If you're serious about it, come back tomorrow, and then the next day and the next," Laleh said. "I'll teach you."

"You will?" Every part of me was igniting. I didn't know what I wanted more, to be back on a horse or to win her approval.

"Yes, you know why? Because you're a feminist." She winked.

I returned the next day bursting with excitement. Reyhan was nowhere to be found, nor were the other women I had seen the day before—except for Laleh. As she saddled up a different horse, this one a brownish-reddish color I would learn was referred to as "sorrel," Laleh explained that the others were out on a trail ride—or *dasht* as she called it—honing skills she would teach me in time.

We rode in the arena all morning until the noontime sun beat down on our backs. This horse, whose name was Ostad (or "professor"), was like riding in a Cadillac. Even when he trotted, I wasn't jostled. Instead, I floated on a cloud, watching the horizon rise and fall as we rode. Ostad's instincts were impeccable. He knew to begin at a slow pace and then to quicken just so. He picked up the gait, and my heart fluttered. Ostad transitioned from pace to pace effortlessly, slowing and then quickening on the turns and zigzags we took around the farm. Even when I lost my bearings, Ostad remained steady. When I forgot to dig my right heel into his ribs to tell him to turn left, he still turned left to avoid the obstacle course that Laleh and Vida had laid out for me. And it seemed that all I had to do was think a command in my head and Ostad followed it before my body even had a chance to signal, squeeze for speed, or kick for direction.

I returned every day for a week straight. On the seventh day, as I was packing my bag before the sun rose, my aunt stopped me.

"Have you shifted to horses then? No more sexual revolution?" she asked, her perfectly tattooed black eyebrows raised.

"This is just something I have to do for me, *khaleh*. I have a feeling these women might be a different piece of the same puzzle."

My aunt sighed. By this point she had stopped questioning my whereabouts after a series of awkward midnight encounters the summer before when she caught me sneaking back into her apartment—twice with a young man in tow. We agreed that summer on a "don't ask, don't tell" policy that would keep her out of trouble with my parents—and the authorities, should it come to that. And it would keep me free from having to divulge details I wasn't ready to speak aloud quite yet to a family member. But she remained curious about my work. A self-proclaimed feminist who never married, she spent many evenings reading my field notes and helping me think through the sexual revolution unfolding before my very eyes on the streets of Iran.

That morning, as I bumped my tiny Toyota Yaris along the dirt road leading to the horse farm, I decided two things: first, I was ready to leave the arena for the hills, and second, while we rode, I was determined to ask Laleh about her feminism. With each successful lap around the outdoor arena, I felt a developing trust between us. Laleh watched me closely. Occasionally, she would ask about my research, but when I returned the questioning, she would gallop away on her stallion, throwing a mischievous smile across her shoulder.

"I'm ready, Laleh. Today is the day," I announced. She was grooming Ostad out in the pasture. They both turned their heads at the sound of my voice. Ostad followed Laleh obediently as she walked toward me.

"Ha! That's funny. I don't think you're ready," she replied. She shook her head as she drew closer to me. I had to tilt my head to meet her gaze. I wished I was a foot taller or mounted on a horse.

"I *am* ready, dear friend. You have taught me to—"

"There is a whole world of danger out there," she interjected. "You have to be ready for anything."

"Laleh, I am in Iran researching probably the most dangerous topic of all time—sex. I *am* ready for anything. I'm going to ride out there." I pointed toward the trees at the edge of the farm, which led to the mountains. "With or without you." It would take almost two decades for me to realize how much this combination of unexamined fear and draw of danger was wearing on my soul, preventing me even from surrendering to my new passion—riding.

Laleh dug her hands into her hair and shot me an exasperated look.

"Fine. Let's ride."

I didn't have time to wonder if my jaw was broken. The revving of motorbikes had come out of nowhere, shaking my skin from my bones, and it was instinct that pulled my head down just as my horse flung his back. The full force of Ostad's head collided with my face. *Crack*. I turned my head, wincing.

More revving. Ostad let out a loud neigh and reared up on his hind legs, ready for battle. And then the mountain I had been staring at with fierce determination was upside down. Ostad had bucked and I had fallen, but I continued to hold on to his red-and-white woven snaffle.

"Let go!" Laleh shouted, straining to be heard over the brigade of motorbikes. I hadn't seen them, hadn't sensed them coming, nor could I find them now that I was belly up to the sky. I hadn't listened to Laleh. I was still holding the reins as Ostad galloped away. He was dragging me, my back scraping against the rocky soil.

I tried to turn and jackknife my body to pull us both to a halt. But I wasn't a strong enough rider and only succeeded in bellyflopping into the ground. My twisting gave Ostad the slack he needed, and he broke free of my grip. I looked up to see his dark mane blowing in the wind, his tail swishing, as he galloped away leaving a trail of dust behind him.

I had been flying. Only moments before it had been *my* black hair in the wind as we rode up the mountain together. My legs had encircled Ostad's perfectly formed belly, his brown-red fur melting into my heels. When Ostad tossed his mane, I did the same. Now dirt coated the inside of my mouth. Jammed in the crevices of my teeth were flecks of the smooth sandstone rock I had fallen in love with on my first trip into the mountains just a few months earlier. I lay flat on my back, not moving. I moved my tongue first to the right then to the left, and, neither direction felt like a good idea. My jaw might well be broken. I tried to spit, failed, and lay back down.

If I could have remained forever lying in that field, my bleeding scalp irrigating the wildflowers that sprung up at the base of Mount Damavand, I would have. I wanted to close my eyes, to feel the sun kiss my cheeks, to inhale the intoxicating scent of lavender and the aromatic dirt that I hungered for whenever I was in the city. But the roar of revving engines pulverized my peace, and my eyes met Laleh's. She was still on her shimmering black stallion, Felfel. Her horse was the picture of calm. She squeezed gently with only the tips of her fingers, and he came to a halt.

"Pardis! Get up, now!" Laleh was less calm. Her brownish-red hair started peeking out from the headscarf she had clearly tried to quickly yank back up when the bikers arrived. Her face was flushed. She looked over her shoulder.

I managed to push myself up onto my elbows, and that was when I finally saw them. Five bearded men on motorcycles riding in a V formation. The man at the front wore aviator glasses and a green cloth tied around his neck. The others wore a green cloth tied around their heads. I would later learn that this was a sign of Shia would-be martyrs. I scanned the horizon for Reyhan. But when I heard her voice, it came from behind me.

"They're Revolutionary Guards. We gotta go!" Reyhan called out. It was as if she had materialized out of thin air. Laleh and I had been riding for two hours, trying to catch up to her and the others with no luck, and yet now here she was, just in time to see my *spectacular* failure. I heard the familiar drumming of Ostad's hooves, and I spun around. Reyhan, atop her glowing white mare, Tala, was pounding toward me, the red-and-white woven reins in her hand. She had managed to corral Ostad and was leading him by the muzzle as she galloped toward the spot where Laleh and her horse had me encircled.

I tried to stand but my body betrayed me; it was not yet ready to get back on the horse.

"We don't have time, Pardis. Get up and get on!" Reyhan screamed. Her perfectly rounded lips were pulled back to highlight the fang-like shape of her upper molars. My body stayed firmly rooted to the soil.

"I told you that you need to learn to walk before you can run," Laleh tsked. "But you insisted you were ready, insisted you wanted to go for a *dasht* up in the hills. Now prove to me you can do it. Get up and be the Persian warrior woman you are."

Her words sent a jolt through my body. *Persian warrior woman*. Gordafarid, the Persian warrior princess, had inspired me to climb onto a horse in the first place. Laleh's eyes burned into mine. A mix of anger, desperation, and terror locked us together.

I didn't know what hurt more—my jaw, my ribs, or my ego. Just moments earlier I had felt so confident, so free, so much at *home* riding through the hills of my native homeland on a horse who seemed to understand me better than any human ever had. But I had been caught up in the idea of my riding, in picturing what I must have looked like to Laleh, in thinking about the stories I would tell my friends and family back home about how I found belonging inside of equine adrenaline as I careened through the mountains and valleys of Iran. I was so fixated on my past and future that I hadn't focused on the present and had disconnected from Ostad, who had no doubt tried to warn me with his quickening pace.

"Are you a feminist warrior or are you afraid?" she screamed.

I CAME TO MY ANCESTRAL HOME expecting to fall in love
with Iran. And I did. But then I fell for Persia. Iran was the shimmering lights, the opulence of parties, the tense passions between sex and politics. Persia was the smell of olive trees mixed
with the mist of the Caspian Sea, the roadside villages where
women washed clothes and dishes in open ditches of tumbling
water that wound their way through a lush green landscape.

My mind was in Iran, but my heart was in Persia. Each seduced me in a different way. Learning to ride was my love affair
with Persia. I wanted more—of both. I was young, hungry, and
greedy. I wasn't ready to give up one for the other.

On my way to three-day raves in the northern part of the
country, I would stop to ride with Laleh and her friends in the
moss-covered steppe plains that frame the Caspian Sea. They
had decamped to the north to escape the summer heat and in
search of longer rides. We rode through small villages where
horse-drawn carriages still outnumbered cars, and I smiled

at the children splashing in the creeks and open sewers—or *juubs*—that wound their way along the roadside. Olive trees provided shade along the village paths and gave way to open rice paddies, where women worked with babies tied to their backs.

As we rode the familiar road toward the rolling green hills that surrounded the Caspian, Laleh told me the story of the extraordinary breeds of horses we were riding and their lineage—which was our lineage too. "The oldest horses on record to date, originated in Persia," she told me with great excitement, "and have been memorialized in carvings and hieroglyphics for thousands of years." She told me about her favorite breeds like Akhal-Teke, Caspians, and other mixes. I became enchanted with the story of the Caspian the more Laleh spoke about them.

She told me that these horses were the same ones whose images were emblazoned on the walls of Persepolis, depicting the great triumphs of the Persian empire. And through time these same horses had helped our people find their way and make history. The story of the Caspian horse is the story of empire. It is also the story of our people, of the strength that carried us through and propelled us forward.

When I wasn't riding, I devoured everything I could find about the Caspian horse: what its legacy was, how Caspian horses were made for the shifting terrain, how their calm yet fierce temperament was the perfect complement to my people. Caspian horses, I learned, had survived thousands of years because of their combination of adaptability, intellect, and the ability to surrender to and be curious about their changing surroundings. As humans built palaces, replaced dirt roads with cobblestone streets, and paved pathways, Caspian horses learned to walk on the shifting terrain rather than refusing to trod on unknown footing. For these reasons and more, my ancestors had continued to choose Caspian horses over other breeds like Arabians, Turkomans, or Akhal-Tekes—even sometimes crossbreeding them—to help them build their civilizations. Caspians were a source of inspiration and wonder to Persians for thousands of years, just as they had become for me. And the poems, stories, and paintings of the horses throughout history revealed the reverence my ancestors had for these animals. They bowed to them, cited Caspian horses as the gateway to heaven, and wrote that there was nothing a human could do to be closer to God than to care for and surrender to a horse. This last phrase, a quote attributed to the Persian Sufi mystic Jalaluddin Rumi, was carved into the walls of the farmhouse in Kordan where I was learning to ride.

While I was spending most of my time in Iran between 2000 and 2007, I continued to make regular trips back "home" to the United States to ensure my doctoral studies at Columbia remained on track. On occasion, I would also return to California to see my family, and during these visits, I sought out the company of horses. But riding in Southern California was nothing like riding in Iran. In fact, it felt quite the opposite. Rather than riding as free surrender, the way I had been drawn to by watching riders in Iran, the trainers in San Diego wanted me to ride only in tight circles with as much control over the horses as possible. Instead of releasing my hips to sway with the motion of the horse, as Reyhan and Laleh had done, the trainers gripped them with the full force of their quadriceps and thighs, unwilling to let go. My Iranian teachers had emphasized that I shouldn't try to steer the horse in circles, but rather let him choose the direction and path and only steer or intervene if danger was on the horizon. "Let them choose the path," Reyhan repeated to me. "The horses know the way better than you." But in the United States, at least in the arenas I found my way to, it was the opposite. I was told to clutch the reins mercilessly, to keep a tight grip on the horses' faces, and I was handed a crop to whip their hind ends when they misbehaved. The tightness of the Californian trainers' bodies was rivaled only by their set jaws, gritted teeth, and angry commands atop the equines. This was the opposite of surrender, the opposite of freedom. It felt unnatural. The attempt to dominate a majestic creature that has dominated history felt all wrong.

I left the arenas of San Diego in search instead of trail rides in the canyons of California and Utah. But there I was met with still further disappointment. The trail horses kept by outfitters in the Southwest appeared soulless. They had been so badly broken by their owners. Commanded for years to ride with their noses almost glued to the tail of the horse in front of them, their heads didn't bob with joy, nor did their ears wiggle with curiosity. They were resigned to a fate of indentured servitude. And they hardly noticed if anyone was riding them or not. Furthermore, riding these horses—Quarter Horses, I was told—made my hips sore; their round torsos didn't fit my body. My spine ached with their rough hoofbeat, which I would later learn was because they were not gaited, meaning that their legs did not move symmetrically but instead jumped front and then back like a jackrabbit's. The ride was choppy, causing pain to shimmy throughout my bones rather than adrenaline.

Worse still, the camaraderie of riding was missing. Whether I was trail riding or confined to the arena, none of the women riding with or around me were interested in connecting. They were laser focused on themselves and their horses, not recognizing how herd-bound these animals are, how herd-bound *we* are. Instead of friendship, many of the other women—barn witches, I later learned they were called—wanted only to compare, to judge. They narrowed their eyes at me as I rode, looking for faults so they could feel superior. This only made my fear of falling worse. I was determined to prove them wrong. And this determination, coupled with the tight-lipped women who vowed to never surrender, began stripping me of the joy that riding had brought me in Iran.

Between the horses, the trainers, and the barn witches, I soon gave up riding in California altogether. I decided that riding was best saved for the Middle East, the cradle of civilization and the home of the oldest living horse breed on record. If it meant months at a time without a horse between my legs, so be it. I decided I would rather wait until my return to my ancestral homeland to ride than try to make my body and spirit fit what felt like a foreign riding world.

In contrast to Western horses, Iranian horses felt like gliding in a rocking chair. My body clicked with theirs, my legs wrapping comfortably around their cylindrical midsections. And the way their shoulders moved their legs, like the ballerinas I had watched at Lincoln Center in New York, made the ride more flying than bouncing.

By the summer of 2006, when I returned to Iran after six long months in the United States, Laleh had connected with a different group of women who managed a stable on the Turkish-Iranian border. They rode Caspian and Turkoman horses and bred both throughout Turkey. They had a unique approach to horses, a type of horsewomanship, as they called it, that was about communicating with the animals rather than trying to discipline or dominate them. Ahu, whose name meant "gazelle" and which fit her perfectly, was a trainer who owned a herd of horses in Shahpur. She invited Laleh and me to join her for a ride across the Turkish border. We could hardly wait.

When we arrived in Shahpur, we were overwhelmed by the beauty of Ahu's herd. Four dozen or more horses were running in the lush green pastures of her farm, throwing their manes and twirling their tails as they frolicked freely in the velvety grass. My jaw fell open as I watched them run, twist, jump, and play, their muscles flexing and glistening in the sun. A dozen women were also frolicking among the olive and mulberry trees. Ahu introduced me to them all. They nodded and smiled. I watched as two of them held a bedsheet under a mulberry tree and two more climbed up the branches to shake the berries loose. Everyone squealed in delight as the fruit rained down.

Ahu's talents as a trainer were self-evident. She showed me how to create mutual trust and respect with the horses from my very first interaction with them. She would look a horse in the eye and bow by placing her right leg behind her left and lowering herself, like a curtsy. As knee met ground, she would lower her eyes, place her left hand on her left knee, and drop her right hand. The horses would then bow to her. Then and only then, when the connection was established, would she groom and saddle them. I learned to do the same.

"You bring trust so you can surrender. And only when you truly surrender can you feel the fullness of the joy of riding," Ahu would tell me. It took me years to understand this lesson.

Barely five feet tall, Ahu, with her hair in French braids, had perfectly round eyes that matched the roundness of her red-headed mare, Setareh. The horse was smaller than the others, but she had a larger head that she held high. I later learned that this horse could not carry a rider who weighed more than one hundred pounds. Ahu and Setareh were a perfect fit for each other.

Like Laleh and Reyhan, Ahu rode in a saddle made of brilliantly colored fabrics. She fastened two pillow-like blankets onto her mare with two pieces of blue-and-yellow chiffon fabric that matched the turquoise-and-yellow pattern of her headscarf. She made a kissing sound, and the other women on the farm gathered around her to receive their orders. Ahu looked each of the women up and down, and then turned her gaze toward Laleh and me. Her delicate brows furrowed as she considered each of our bodies to determine the right equine match for us. One after the other, she called out names. As the women heard their names and that of their assigned horses, they peeled off effortlessly, gliding toward the stables, grinning from ear to ear, and returning with their own piles of fabric, pillow blankets, and woven reins.

Laleh was kind enough to fasten my blanket-saddle for me when I met my stunning gelding. She helped me up and onto his back, and we were all off, galloping into the wind, laughing, singing, and bouncing in tune with the perfect rhythms of hoofbeats. I let my hips and body go, fusing with the animal between my thighs. For a moment, I left my fear of falling behind and surrendered to the moment. It was the first time I felt the joy of surrender pour into and then out of me.

As soon as we crossed over the Iranian border and hit the open trails of the Turkish countryside, every one of the women tore off their headscarves and shook out their hair. The horses followed suit, tossing their thick, bushy manes.

"*Azaadi!* Freedom!" they shouted. And I felt that freedom in my every bone. Open terrain, beckoning mountains, and elegant, graceful horses. This riding felt effortless. Rather than trying to control, restrict, and tighten the movements of the horse and in turn my own body, as the California trainers insisted, this was about melting into the horse, about letting go. It was about letting my hips flow in a figure eight, a side-to-side swish—not unlike the snake-slithering movements Persian dance called for. Be in tune *with* the horses, release the death grip on the reins, trust them.

We galloped into the hills, hooves barely grazing the ground beneath us. As we rode, I learned that Ahu and her team trained women to fight, shoot, and prepare for combat—all on horseback.

"Our horses are our survival in more ways than one, but they also make us vulnerable to society," Ahu told me as we pounded farther up into the mountains.

Rhana, another of the horsewomen, joined our conversation. "Look, Pardis, what you write about how young people in Tehran are doing what they aren't supposed to be doing with their bodies—well, that's us, too. Women aren't supposed to be straddling a horse. They think we lose our hymens this way, for whatever that's worth." Rhana was the tallest of the riders and thus rode the largest horse, a beautiful Akhal-Teke, descended from the Turkoman horse, with a metallic white sheen that stood in sharp contrast to Rhana's almost glowingly black hair. Rhana and her horse commanded attention. Like Reyhan, when Rhana rode, she dropped the reins and turned her palms up to the sky. I watched as she closed her eyes, a smile taking over her entire body as she lifted her face up to bask in the sun.

"Riding makes us vulnerable because we are doing something 'un-Islamic,'" Ahu continued. "But riding also gives us freedom. A way out. A way and a place to surrender to nature, to animals, to God and the universe. Our every move is restricted in Tehran. But not when we are mounted. We can ride into the mountains, into the caves where the women are training. Training to fight anyone who dares come to tell us what we can or can't do."

"Riding also is our survival because it is the only place where we can be truly free. Where we can surrender to love, joy, and beauty," Rhana added. She didn't open her eyes to speak. Rather, she continued surrendering to her horse, letting her hips move with his shoulders as she glided through the air.

This was their quiet revolution: engaging in behaviors deemed un-Islamic and relishing the power of their own choices. Unwilling to be controlled by a regime with which they did not agree, they used their bodies, actions, and choices to speak back. If mandated to wear a headscarf, they slid it back one millimeter at a time until it was gone altogether. If threatened with arrest and invasive virginity testing for being in public with a man they were not married to, or for riding a bike or a horse, they did so defiantly in order to send a message: the regime be damned—they would not be tamed. These women, more so than me, lived in a world of danger. But rather than succumb to fear or let the adrenaline of danger take over their lives, they chose to surrender to riding. This was how they kept themselves safe and sane. This was how they nourished their spirits. And everything they did punctuated their philosophies. They preferred the company of women and horses to others in the country. When they weren't training or breeding horses for upper-class diplomats, they spent every waking moment in the mountains training and plotting. They were preparing for the day when the Islamic Republic was finally going to be challenged— they knew it was coming. They were going to be a part of the revolution. A revolution led by women refusing to be controlled by patriarchal interpretations of spirituality. A movement where women's bodies would unseat the mullahs, challenging one of the most elusive and oppressive regimes of our time.

I spent the next week learning the intricate details of their horsewomanship as we made camp in a small village in Turkey. In certain parts of the world, I discovered, this is referred to by some as "feminist riding." The principles were similar to what I had been told by the women I met in Kordan: Begin by communicating with your horse. Make sure he is locked into you and trusts you completely. Just as the horses are the riders' survival, so too are the riders the horse's survival. The horse depends on the rider. When out on the trail, in the mountains, in unfamiliar terrain, the familiarity of the relationship between rider and horse will keep the horses calm and the riders safe. Surrender to the horse and he will surrender to you. Communicating clearly, giving the correct signals, and anticipating danger rather than seeking it out keeps everyone safe. Be in harmony with your horse and with the earth around you, I was told over and over.

Surrender. Anticipate danger. But don't let your fears go unexamined. Their words danced inside me.

Ahu showed me how to teach my horse not to fear the unknown. If he jumped at the sound of a car door slamming, we would walk him over to the car and slam the door over and over again until he was unfazed. And the trick to "desensitization" as she called it was letting the horse rest next to what he feared most. She taught me to run the horse hard in areas where he was comfortable and then to walk him next to something he feared—a sound like a car door or even running water or crossing a bridge. When we got to the unknown thing that brought fear into his heart, we let him rest, catch his breath, and we stood with him calmly. Slowly, over time, the horse learned to associate the thing he feared with rest and relaxation—that which he craved most. This was a way to combat the adrenaline that made a horse bolt, buck, or rear.

"Have him face his fears, not be driven by them. That way he won't hurt you or himself," Ahu explained. Later in life I would have to teach myself the same lesson.

"How do you know he has relaxed?" I asked.

"Lock into him. See? He licks his lips and relaxes his right foot when you make eye contact. That's how I know he is relaxed. And he does that a lot with you."

She sensed a growing bond between me and Baran, the brown gelding with the black mane I had been assigned during our first ride across the border, so he became my horse.

"His name means 'rain' in English." I smiled. My heart skipped a beat when I thought about this elegant creature as a rainmaker.

"I kind of think of you that way, Pardis," Laleh said. "You're a rainmaker too. Powerful energy follows you both. So you're well matched."

When I sat on Baran I felt his body suture with mine. The energy coursed between us. I wanted to squeeze and then release my legs and go galloping into the sky bareback and rein-free, catching the wind in my hair.

"You're not ready yet." Ahu read my mind. She handed me the woven red-and-white reins. I started to choke up on them, curling my fingers tightly around the yarn. Ahu stopped me again.

"Surrender. That means let go. Don't grip his body with yours, don't pull on his face with your hands."

I nodded slowly. I had to fight every instinct to hold on for dear life, had to eschew the lessons from California where teachers insisted I choke up on the reins, making sure I had the horse's mouth in my grips at all times.

"Soft hands, Pardis, soft hands, soft body. Let go," Ahu lectured. "The harder you squeeze, the harder he will fight back. Remember, horses don't respond to pressure; they respond to the *absence* of pressure. So you can't condition them by constantly yanking on them, squeezing them, trying to pull them in. When you do that, you are teaching him to pull back harder. The horse only remembers the last thing you and he did before you let go of the pressure. So if you yank hard on his face or pound on his ribs with your legs, then he will wait until you pound hard and grip tight to do what you want him to do. That is unhealthy for both of you."

I uncurled my fingers slowly, then dropped the reins altogether.

"No, no, no, I didn't say drop them." Ahu laughed. "Here, okay, sister, watch me." Ahu curtsied to Setareh, and she lowered so Ahu could mount effortlessly. She held the very end of the reins loosely between the thumb and middle finger of her right hand. She made a kissing sound so she and Setareh stood facing Baran and I. My heart dropped. I had learned in the United States that two horses should never square off unless you were looking for trouble. But Setareh and Baran were as gentle as ever. There was no hostility between the animals, only curiosity as they sniffed each other's faces.

"Okay, watch, sweet sister." Ahu held the end of the reins in her right hand. With her left hand she pulled slightly to the left while leaning her body to the right. Setareh bent her head all the way around Ahu's leg to kiss her left knee. Then Ahu repeated the same motion to the right: holding the reins with her left middle finger and thumb, pulling with the right hand ever so subtly, and leaning left. Setareh turned to kiss her right knee.

Now it was my turn. I thought I was doing exactly what I had just watched my new teacher do, but Baran didn't move.

"You need to give him slack with the right if you are pulling with the left, sister. He needs somewhere to go." Ahu laughed.

It took several more hours, several muscles cramping, and a sore bottom as I fought the urge to clench my buttocks as the American riders did. But after a few days I finally started to understand the method. Leave the reins loose but hold them delicately in case you need to communicate with your horse. Use your legs to guide him gently. Squeeze, don't kick. Pull gently, don't yank. Enter a meditative state. Let that be what is seductive—meditative relaxation—not adrenaline or the thrill of danger. I was starting to let go.

On the seventh day, Ahu took me for a ride out to a nearby lake. I was finally ready to ride into the hills bareback, but Ahu insisted I still use my reins. As she and Laleh climbed up on their horses saddle-free and rein-free, I shook my head. I was determined to prove to them that I could ride as they did. My pride was taking over me again, along with a hunger for danger, that familiar codependency with unexamined fear creeping into my soul. Laleh and Ahu began riding. At the last second, I dropped the reins, insisting I was ready to steer with my legs and my abdominals, using Baran's mane as a place to hold on. Baran galloped after Setareh and Aloo, Laleh's assigned horse, tossing his head fiercely. As he picked up speed outside the farm gates, I exhaled a split second of fear and inhaled joy, buoyed by my horse and the countryside.

We galloped past several farms before coming upon a creek. That was when Ahu turned her head to look back and realized that I was riding barefoot, bareback, and bit-free.

"Where are your reins?" she shouted over her shoulder. I could barely hear her over the rushing sound of the creek and Baran's hoofbeats.

"I don't need them!" I called back. I leaned forward, squeezing my legs harder, egging Baran on.

"You. Are. Not. Ready." I could see Ahu's gritted teeth and a fear that fueled her anger with me. But I was determined to prove her wrong.

Forgetting all of my lessons, I kicked Baran's ribs even harder, leaning forward in a dominating position. Baran pounded forward, past Ahu, Laleh, and their horses, who had slowed down to match Ahu's simmer. We were coming up on the creek, and I knew we could ride through the water as we had done on the first border crossing into Turkey. But what I hadn't realized was that a water crossing is very different without a saddle or reins. And while the glistening creek beckoned with a soft whisper, an uneven, rocky terrain sat just beneath the gentle rolling water. We had desensitized Baran to water during our practices, but now my adrenaline was spilling out into him, and I felt his heartbeat quickening to match my pulse.

"Stooooop. *Iiiiist!*" Ahu and Laleh called out. But I didn't listen. Didn't even think to slow down to cross with care. I was determined to show them my bravery, to be the horsewoman warrior who animated my dreams.

As soon as Baran's feet met the water, his hooves began slipping. He lost his footing at the same time I lost my grip on his mane. His shoulder popped right and his hind legs shifted left, and before I knew it, I was soaking wet, the jagged rocks at the bottom of the creek piercing my back. My horse had bucked me, throwing me off to save himself—an act I would later learn to appreciate. Baran splashed to the other side of the water. I looked up to see Laleh and Ahu, their expressions a bemused "I told you so."

Once they realized I wasn't hurt, we all burst into laughter.

"You just don't know when to stop do you, sex doctor?" Laleh giggled. I clutched my dripping wet middle as I laughed and shook my head.

"She really doesn't," Ahu mused. "But she will learn. The horses will teach her."

3   Halt(ed)

YOU JUST DON'T KNOW WHEN TO STOP. Laleh had said it
lightly, but her words stuck with me. I couldn't shake them.
She was right on many levels. I hadn't known, hadn't wanted
to know, when to stop Baran before he catapulted me into the
creek. I rode forward with a reckless fury, determined to prove
that I was indeed a horsewoman warrior. Ready or not, I would
pound forward. And then I fell. And while the cool water in the
creek and the melodious sound of Ahu's and Laleh's laughter
soothed my fall, I should have heeded the lesson. Slow down.
Stop. Assess your surroundings and intentionally surrender to
a different path. But still, I did not.

I returned to the United States and poured myself into my
writing, not stopping to reflect on the lessons I had learned or
the consequences that my research, once made public, might
bring. I finished my dissertation and published my first book:
Passionate Uprisings: Iran's Sexual Revolution. The book was

a celebration of young Iranians' bravery and an overt critique of the senseless ruthlessness of the regime. I told myself I was being fearless by speaking truth to power. That same mix of pride and danger that fueled me forward clouded my ability to pause, stop, reflect. That adrenaline addiction, and the desire to dominate my own story, was slowly eating away at my soul and wearing me down. By telling the regime what they needed to hear about their shortcomings and how a sexual-revolution-fueled youth movement was coming for them, I knew I was endangering myself, but this only propelled me forward. And when my colleagues in Iran invited me to present my findings and the book at Tehran University, I accepted without a second thought.

But I should have halted. I should have seen that the shifting sands of the regime caused uneven terrain that might be treacherous. "Stop. *Iist.*" I heard Ahu's and Laleh's voices in my head. But like that day at the river, I kicked away the warnings and pounded forward. I arrived in Tehran only to meet members of the morality police, who held me in airport detention as soon as I deplaned. They released me the following morning. The detention should have been warning enough, like the sound of Ahu begging me to stop, but again I didn't heed it.

Instead, I dove back into my research on Iran's sexual revolution with a renewed voracity. My desire to challenge the regime, to prove them wrong, to fight for the rights of the people, burned inside me, igniting a fire that clouded my judgment. I did not heed the warnings of my teachers to ensure my phone wasn't tapped. I didn't watch to see who was following me into the emboldened corners of the movement, didn't realize who I was putting at risk. My friends partied with a hungry fury now that was contagious. They were growing increasingly weary of the regime's oppression. And this was coupled with the crippling effect of global sanctions that caused a 45 percent unemployment rate, soaring gas prices, and a crumbling infrastructure. "We sustain ourselves on ideas of freedom," Rhana wrote me in a text message the night I arrived in June 2007. "But ideas don't fill our bellies. And hunger eats away at us."

Many nights people raved as they raged, their rage betraying the effects of a disappointed love of their country. In the afternoons, feminists gathered to strategize ways to dismantle the regime. In the evenings, they and I would lose ourselves in substances that numbed our pain. I was so wrapped up in the movement, I kept ignoring the echoes of Laleh's and Ahu's calls in my head, telling me to slow down. One evening, after a particularly harrowing escape from a party raided by the morality police—whom I later learned had discovered the party because they were following me in an attempt to find ways to charge and arrest me—I decided I needed to get out of Tehran for a while. I called Ahu and made plans to visit her after my lecture at Tehran University, which was scheduled for the following day. I didn't know it then, but that was the last time I would ever hear Ahu's silky voice.

The auditorium smelled of rosin and rosewater as the audience took their seats in the university lecture hall. I was anxious, unsettled; some small part of me wanted to stop, to refuse to walk on stage and speak openly about how sex could unseat the mullahs. But a larger part of me was determined to pound forward, harder, with reckless abandon. I stood at the lectern, gripping the sides of the podium the way I had gripped Baran's legs when I charged into the creek. I took a deep breath and began my critique, knowing, even welcoming, the danger ahead. The regime had failed, I attested. "They let down their people, but the people are rising, bringing a feminist revolution," I roared from the podium. The auditorium doors banged open, and a group of Revolutionary Guards stormed through, ushering in pandemonium. My heart sank, just as it had that day at the creek. But this time there was no soothing sound of my friends' laughter, no neighing of horses to put my soul at ease.

I was halted thirteen minutes into my lecture about sexual politics at Tehran University. I was told I was being charged with the crime of trying to foment a velvet revolution, treason, and being a threat to the Islamic Republic. All because I dared criticize the regime for oppressing its people, for unequal treatment of men and women, for abandoning the true needs of Iranians. I felt myself slowly losing my mind when I was told I couldn't leave the country. Would I die here? Would I ever get out of Iran? Would this painful fall ever stop?

At the end of thirty-three harrowing days, I was put on a plane and told never to return. Three days later, I arrived in the United States a very different woman from the one who had left a few months earlier.

A few weeks after my return to the United States following the ordeal in Tehran, I was still disoriented and moving through my days in a fog of PTSD, unable to pause and reflect. I was determined to get back on my feet, dust myself off, and get back to life as though nothing had happened. I could not show anyone that I had failed. Could not admit the fear that had gripped me when I was under house arrest, the same fear that still had a hold on me, but now it was fear of succumbing to my grief, worries of failure, and the possibility that I might never be the same.

I was determined to do more in every way: To succeed professionally and not let my pain get the better of me. To not surrender to my pain so I could work through it, to rather dominate my emotions. As such, I took on more teaching, added more students, and began applying furiously for grants to return to Iran, not realizing that I really could not return. I refused to talk about my expulsion, hiding it from friends and colleagues in Claremont, where I had been living and teaching at a small liberal arts college. I ignored my family's messages, their desperate calls for me to slow down and take some time to process what had happened to me.

On the eve of my birthday, I got a call from a friend living in New York who had been an old flame during my time in Iran. He had arranged for me to go horseback riding on the beaches of Santa Barbara for my birthday. He knew, better than anyone, that horses were the one thing that could heal me.

"But I hate riding in the United States," I protested.

He sighed. "It's something, Pardis." He had heard of my turmoil, and my close friends in New York City had reported to him that I was falling into a deep depression. I could hear the hope draining from his voice, which made my heart twinge. What he didn't say was that I would never ride in Iran again, but we were both thinking it.

"It's a nice offer, I appreciate it," I said. "I just don't like riding with others out here. It doesn't make sense."

"Then you can ask them to go out alone. We can pay extra for that. Please. Ride alone. I don't care. Just please ride."

As he spoke, I could almost smell the enchanting aroma of horse fur entwined with freshly barreled hay. I closed my eyes and thought about the first time I nuzzled Jahan's snout, inhaling his scent into my body. Riding in California would be no substitute for riding in Iran. But Iran had been taken from me. Laleh. Reyhan. Ahu. All gone. Never again to feel a Caspian or Akhal-Teke between my thighs, never again to weave my fingers through Baran or Jahan's thick mane, floating on his back, flying through the Iranian countryside.

Before I knew it, salty tears filled my eyes. I tried to choke them back, but my friend could hear my pain even through the phone. It was the first time I let myself cry in months.

Fear, disappointment, and determination filled me. I was worried my emotions were going to overwhelm me, and I was disappointed in my inability to hold them back. I wiped away the tears and gritted my teeth, determined to keep moving forward.

"Thank you for the gift," I said, my voice no longer carrying a hint of grief. "I'll ride tomorrow, but I need to ride alone. I don't have time for any judgment from barn witches and certainly don't need photo-obsessed tourists on a trail ride with me."

"Just ride, Pardis. Just ride."

The next morning, I awoke with a giddiness I hadn't felt since my time in Iran. It was my birthday. To be sure, that had something to do with it, but I had dreamed of flying on horseback all night and couldn't wait to be mounted again. I made the two-hour drive to Santa Barbara, my heart pounding the entire way.

As soon as I pulled into the ranch, the skies clouded over, and droplets of rain began covering the fertile soil. I looked up to see a tall brunette with a pixie cut walking my way, her hand over her face to shield her eyes from the rain.

"Ah, you must be Pardis," she said, her voice several octaves higher than I would have predicted, assessing her age to be about fifty-five. She stretched out a hand to shake mine, smiling.

We exchanged pleasantries, and I told her that I wanted to ride out to the beach alone.

"That's not a great idea, especially not today," she said. "As you can see, there is a storm coming. And the ocean is unpredictable."

"I drove a long way to be here," I said. I heard a tense edge in my own voice but decided it was determination rather than trepidation. "Plus, it's my birthday. Are you saying I *can't* ride?"

"First, happy birthday," she said. She pulled me into her office, which was adjacent to the barn. As she spoke, she fished out a raincoat for me to wear and one for herself. "Second, I'm not saying you *can't* ride. Just that it's not a good idea. Especially not alone. But your friend did call to make arrangements and we did agree, so I will leave it up to you. If it were me, I wouldn't ride today. Just take a day off."

I looked at her quizzically. Clearly this woman did not know me. I never allowed myself a day off. I slipped the stiff green poncho over my head and wandered over to the boot section of her office in search of galoshes. My leather boots were no match for this weather.

"I'm going to ride," I announced. The woman took a deep breath and exhaled audibly, her sigh a mix of annoyance and confusion. She shook her head and then pulled out a pair of rubber boots from under her desk that were just my size.

"You'll need a good horse, then. And a lot of luck."

"I will need a good horse. A gelding preferably," I said. I tugged on the boots and followed her to the barn. My heart twinged. I was secretly hoping that Baran or Laleh would be in there waiting for me. That I knew this was an impossibility only made it worse.

"Ah, you prefer the boys, huh?" she said, and I thought I saw her lips curl into a slight smile.

"Mares are lovely, don't get me wrong," I replied. I sensed her preference and didn't want to offend her any more than I already had.

"I get it. Mares are great—I prefer them actually—but they are temperamental. I like them, because I like a challenge," she said.

"I'll take a mare then," I replied. I was never one to back down from a challenge, even one so trite as this. I preferred geldings and knew I would have done better on one that day, but there was no way I was going to let that slide.

"Right then. Glad to hear it." I wasn't sure if it was my imagination or if she was actually looking at me differently now. "I do have a lovely Appaloosa/Arabian mix mare for you if you would like. I think your friend mentioned you ride in Iran. I'm thinking that an Appaloosa/Arabian mix is going to be closer to what you are used to than any of my Quarter Horses."

I nodded gratefully. Perhaps I had misjudged this woman.

She led me through the barn, past large draft horses, Clydesdales with plate-sized hooves, wide-bodied Quarter Horses, until, in the last stall, we came upon a light-brown horse with a long, curling black mane. She was narrower in the body than the rest but had long, thin legs. Her eyelids were half closed as she munched on some hay. A few flecks fell lazily from her mouth. She seemed completely unfazed by our appearance in her stall.

"This is Butterfly," she announced. I should have asked how Butterfly got her name, but I would learn soon enough.

With the barn manager's help, I looped the halter around Butterfly's face and pulled the lead rope around her neck. I still marveled at how technical the equipment in the United States was. Clasps, contouring ropes, metal stirrups hanging from leather. Tack that calloused my hands and made my skin tear. In Iran, everything was fabric and ropes tied in shapes. My fingers would never get used to the struggle with clipping, unclipping, and tightening belt-like cinches. I longed for the chiffon scarves that my friends had used to fasten their soft pillow-blankets.

By the time Butterfly was tacked up and I was mounted, the skies were pouring out fiercely. I shifted uncomfortably in the leather saddle, my thighs searching for the mare's muscles. I could hardly feel the horse through this thick saddle. I did a few stretches with Butterfly inside the barn, twisting my torso and then hers and shifting my legs in search of contact points with her body. I found them as my lower calves and ankles met her rib cage.

"She is very responsive on her ribs," the barn manager said. She was watching me stretch and prepare for the ride. I could see the worry on her face as the rain pounded harder on the roof of the barn. "Just kick hard there, and yank on her face to stop."

Everything she was saying was counterintuitive. Or at least counter to how I had been taught. Laleh and Ahu had stressed that I should never pull too hard on a horse's face, because the harder I pulled, the more desensitized the horse became. And the same went for kicking. So, while I had developed the subtle inner thigh muscles to gently turn, my calves and ankles, and certainly my hands and arms, were not nearly as strong as they perhaps needed to be. For a moment I considered whether I should be riding this particular horse in these conditions. But I would not back down. I was already mounted and sensed I was beginning to earn the respect of this barn manager. I clicked the chin strap of the helmet she insisted I wear, nodded to the woman and dug my heels into Butterfly's ribs to encourage her to walk out of the barn and off the ranch.

Butterfly was hesitant at first. Sheets of rain soaked her mane and tail. She shook her head and turned back toward the barn. I knew from Laleh that a horse going back to the barn meant that I was losing control. I leaned forward, as I had been taught to do, and squeezed my thighs. Butterfly stopped dead in her tracks. The hesitation was all I needed. I kicked her ribs with my heels, acutely aware that the barn manager was watching me. I was determined to prove my skills to her. That was all Butterfly needed. She took off from a trot to a canter to a gallop within seconds, and we were off.

I was flying again. My heart soared, but fear and worry kept creeping into my soul. I pushed them out of my mind, kicking more fiercely, riding harder, faster, faster. I pounded forward, riding through my pain and the longing I felt for my homeland. I started to feel the weight of my exile, my jaw tightening as I considered the gravity of my new reality. I could never return to my ancestral homeland. Would never again ride across the hills of Persia that I had fallen in love with. Never lose myself in conversation with Laleh, Ahu, and the others. The grief gripped me, and I gripped Butterfly's torso even harder—doing exactly what I had been taught not to do, forcing her through a wooded clearing that I knew led to the beach.

A deafening roar filled my ears. I could hear water pounding from all sides. The rain had not let up, and now I could hear the crash of the ocean waves on the beach. I wasn't sure if I was sensing Butterfly's fear or she mine, but as we rode toward the ocean my heart tightened. The rain was coming down so hard and the waves crashing up so high I could barely see.

"Don't stop, Butterfly," I screamed into the sky. I leaned farther forward, squeezed harder, gripping with my entire body. "Don't you dare halt. Ride on," I commanded.

But the mare had heard me utter the magic word. Halt. The word she had been longing to hear since we left the barn. And that was all she needed. She pulled to an abrupt halt, not bothering to slow from her gallop to a trot to a walk. As she dug her heels into the wet sand I went flying forward off Butterfly, landing with a thud on my left shoulder. The wet reins fell from my hands instantly. As I lay on the sand clutching my shoulder, I watched Butterfly rear up to look down at me from her hind legs. She circled her two front hooves in a show of her power. But when her front feet came down, I noticed she was sinking. And then I realized I was sinking, too. Had we ridden into quicksand? We were both halted now. I had failed another lesson. I had not been there for her, had not looked out for my horse. And so, I had lost her trust and broken any communicative bond we had been forming. Our eyes met, and I could almost hear her telling me what my friends and family had been saying for months.

You need to slow down. You need to halt. Or life will do it for you.

We were both sinking into the earth now. Butterfly panicked as she tried but failed to rear again. Finally, she got her hooves free and galloped off at top speed, the saddle having slid to the underside of her belly, the stirrups dragging behind in the sand. I watched in wonder as she rode back the way we had come, leaving me there on the beach alone, on the ground, in pain.

Before I had the chance to calculate how fast I was sinking in the quicksand, a wave pummeled me. I had been sitting with my legs outstretched, my right hand clutching my left shoulder, which I was hoping was not broken. The wave shot me forward across the beach, and I didn't have the chance to break my fall with either hand, so—for the second time that day—I catapulted face-first into the ground. I swallowed a mouthful of sand as the earth nearly swallowed me whole. I didn't know how my legs got out of the sand they were submerged in, but now I was laying on my belly, drenched from head to toe, trying to find the strength to push myself up to a seat and hopefully a stand.

Years of growing up on the ocean should have taught me that where there is one big wave, surely more are coming behind it. Especially in the midst of a storm that was causing ten-foot swells. I had scarcely pushed up to kneeling when I was knocked forward again. This time I caught myself with my hand as the wave crashed over me. Three more waves came in rhythmic succession. And because I was in physical pain and drained of all energy, I sat motionless, halted. Kneeling into the sand, feeling the water push and pull around me. Sensing the earth below, the sky above, and water coming from all directions.

There was nothing else. Nowhere to go. No other choice. Only stillness.

Walk On

THE DAY I STOOD STILL while the ocean raged over me was the last time I rode a horse for more than a decade. I decided I couldn't ride again until I faced my fears and processed my emotions. And yet I continued to struggle. Some part of me knew I needed to surrender to my pain in order to understand it. Was my rage a disappointed love of country and homeland? Was it anxiety that I would never fit in? A fear of never feeling as good as I did when I rode through the hills of Kordan? Or a combination of all of this? I continued to kick my pain away, attempting to dominate my feelings, refusing to surrender, accept, process, and move on.

Unable to muster the strength to stand up to my Iranian-American community and family, I agreed to a loveless—at least on my end—marriage that lasted less than two years. We married, then divorced, and still, I hardly felt a thing. I had thought that marrying an Iranian man who had recently emigrated would help me feel more connected to the homeland that had expelled me. I hoped that he would bring me back to life. But none of this happened.

Until that point I had been pummeling through what I perceived as a danger-filled world. One where being Iranian American was a threat in both Iran and America. One where being a woman studying sex resulted in a harrowing arrest, detention, and exile. A world where my parents' sacrifice to leave the ancestral homeland in search of safety and a better life for the family exacted a heavy weight on me to succeed at all costs—even if the cost was losing myself. One where I feared falling but still refused to stop riding through life recklessly, trying to dominate. Where I harnessed my fear because that is what I had been taught to do since a young age. Use the fear of danger to fuel you—I had learned this painful coping strategy as a young child—even if it causes you harm. The only option not available is falling, revealing your inner struggle and weakness to the world.

But then I fell. My horse halted and threw me. I was left, sinking, paralyzed by the impact of the fall. And while I got up and returned to my life in California, some part of me remained frozen, halted. I moved almost in spite of myself.

Walk on, I could almost hear Laleh command her horse. I tried to walk on deliberately in my life. Surrendering to the pain in the moments when I could allow it to take me into a place of darkness in my heart. Only in acknowledging and surrendering to my pain could I glimpse a path forward when the darkness of depression threatened to be my undoing.

My husband and I divorced while I was pregnant with my first child. It was a harrowing breakup involving pain on many fronts. And still, I kept soldiering forward—almost in a daze.

Not stopping, turning, or backing up to the barn, to safety, to a place to heal. Just walking on. I continued my research with a fervor, winning one, then another and another grant, fellowship, and award. I received tenure and became chair of my department. I catapulted into another marriage, this time to a friend and colleague who promised support, comfort, and love. Part of me wondered if he provided the shelter of a barn for a horse and rider in the storm. And maybe it was this part that led me to make a decision I would regret. We married in 2014. There were interludes of happiness, such as having two more children. My home was filled with love and joy, but still, many of these feelings did not and could not penetrate my mix of rage and grief at the heartbreak my ancestral home gave me. I was walking forward in my life in a fog. Wandering a jagged path, I was aware of the danger and beauty around me but unable to look up, for my gaze, like that of a horse without a trusted rider, was fixed on the ground.

But in 2017, on the tenth anniversary of my arrest and expulsion from my native homeland, I smelled orange blossoms during an unusually cool California summer. July was typically the hottest month in Claremont, but we had been blessed with rains that quenched the unending thirst of the trees lining the streets of the college town. As the jacaranda trees burst their buds into fireworks in all shades of purplish-blue, wafts of citrus infused with the plumeria blew orange blossoms through the wind and onto my tongue. I longed to taste my aunt's orange marmalade on freshly fired bread from the baker in Kordan.

Up to that point 2017 had been a difficult year. A new American president announced his arrival with a vengeance and swore to rid the United States of all threats—and threat number one happened to be my people.

Somehow, Donald Trump and John Bolton's desire to erase Iran actually erased my resistance to Iran. I began thawing out of the numbness that had gripped me since my arrest. For the first time in a decade, I felt a deep love and longing replace the rage and grief for the homeland I had lost. I realized that rage was really love disappointed. I had been disappointed in my ancestral homeland, with which I had fallen in love. But now, I wanted Iran back—or at least I wanted to find my way back to harmony with Iran. It was the only way to survive the fascism we were now living under in the United States. And the irony of the similarities between Trump and the hardliners who kicked me out of Iran didn't elude me.

It was time. Time to dive back in and sort through the memories of Iran. This meant unearthing memories of trauma that I had repressed for over a decade. Allowing the pain in would also allow the joy to permeate through the hardened exterior I had maintained for the past several years. I knew I had to surrender to the pain. Ahu had taught me that in riding. But it hadn't sunk in.

Maybe now I could ride again, too. When I locked Iran away, I had also deprived myself of the joy of horses. With my friend's insistence, I had given riding one last try after my return to the United States, but being catapulted into quicksand had been the final nail in the coffin I'd constructed in my head. I didn't deserve the horses, I told myself. The horses and Iran were fused in my soul. If I couldn't have one, I couldn't have the other. This was among the many after-effects the trauma of interrogation and expulsion had left on my body and brain.

I turned my attention to the effects of intergenerational trauma and the layers of pain I had inherited and experienced. But in 2017, when I finally allowed myself to delve back into my time in Iran, I also reconnected with my paternal family, all of whom were still living there. I began having weekly calls with my relatives, eager to catch up on what was happening in Iran but also hungry for their voices speaking to me in my native tongue, telling me stories about a homeland I ached for. And the sexual revolution had picked up momentum, inspiring protests against the regime that continued to build. By 2017, more people wanted the mullahs out of Iran than in, my relatives told me. Their town of Mashad, a religious capital, was changing. People were in the streets demanding that the regime respect their rights, feed their families, bring prosperity to the country.

I couldn't get enough of Iran—I wanted to call my family and friends every day. So, for the next four years, this is exactly what I did. And it was during these conversations with my elderly aunts and cousins that I learned something I had somehow missed.

My father and aunts had been raised on a farm near the Caspian Sea in the town of Sari. This much I knew. But I didn't know that my grandmother Maryam, my father's mother, had been a horsewoman. And not just any horsewoman but a horsewoman warrior who protected her lands, family, and herd by riding fully armed on horseback. If that weren't inspiring enough, I also learned that she rode Caspian horses, my favorite breed! Maryam had been instrumental in helping to breed them out of extinction. She was fearless, my aunts told me. My father had never wished to speak of his mother, perhaps because her memory was intertwined with an Iran that he had lost. Maybe my father was still wandering in the same frozen walk that had gripped me for the past decade, but his was a life sentence. He wouldn't allow himself to think of his family, his homeland, the loves he had left behind during the revolution.

Listening to the stories of my family, my grandmother, and my aunts, I realized that I had inherited not just pain but strength. And this strength came from surrendering to horses, to nature, and even to their pain. It was true that my parents lived in the pain of exile, a pain that had also paralyzed me for years. But it was equally true that other members of my family had moved through the pain of their experiences—theft, rape, murder—by finding their voices, finding their courage, and using their emotions as *assets*. Their intergenerational strength was also the blood coursing through my veins. A strength that had enabled me to survive the terrible torture of my expulsion and exile. The resilience that made me stand up and get back on the horse after falling the first time I rode outside of Tehran. Now, after ten years, it was time to get back on the horse once more. But this time I would heed the words and lessons of the Iranian horsewomen.

By this point I was living in Phoenix, Arizona, a city that fortunately was home to a wide variety of equines. Finding a barn was easy. Connecting with a horse was not. After six weeks of searching, one of my Iranian-American friends introduced me to an Iranian émigré who owned a barn in Scottsdale. I visited his stables and met the new love of my life, a buckskin Quarter Horse gelding named Ice who I called "Yakh"—the Farsi translation of his name. With perfectly rounded cheeks that made his face look like a friendly stuffed animal, Yakh was smaller than most Quarter Horses, with a rounder head. He reminded me of a Caspian.

Yakh was a young horse, only four years old when I met him in 2020. While his face and eyes were gentle, his spirit was pure fire. The first time I sat on him I felt a jolt of energy flow through me. At the time, I attributed it to the exhilaration of being back on a horse after a decade of deprivation. But I later learned that it was Yakh's energy locking in with mine, an energy that grew as I reflected it back to him. Yakh's body was rounder than the other horses I had ridden. Fortunately, birthing three children had loosened my hips a great deal. But still, I felt a tightness in my thighs and hip sockets as I rode him, realizing I had to widen my straddle. My body ached for the perfectly formed Caspian horses that allowed my legs to dangle delicately. Still, I was on a gem of a horse. And each step he took brought me out of the numbness I had felt for the past decade as depression took hold of me. The pain of exile, the challenge of having three children and two divorces, and the stabbing sense of betrayal by my homeland had been enough to shut off my emotions completely—that and the medication I was given to cope. But now, with the help of Yakh and his energy, I was slowly thawing out.

And Brynn, the trainer at the Scottsdale barn, reminded me a great deal of Ahu. With fierce eyes and a toughness that oozed from every pore, Brynn carried many of the same values as the horsewomen from Iran. I was determined to bond with her.

Day after day, I rose at 5 a.m. so that Yakh and I could ride before the triple-digit heat threatened to burn us both. Brynn, like Ahu, expected a lot of her riders and her horses. Every time

I climbed up on Yakh's withers, I was terrified of letting her—and myself—down. My initial impulse had been to show her my skills by riding hard, going quickly from a walk to a trot to a canter.

"You're not ready to canter now, Pardis," Brynn said as I pounded around the arena, beads of sweat dripping down my and my horse's bodies. "I hate to state the obvious, but you have to walk first. Then we will get to the trot. Then the canter."

"But I galloped through mountains and rivers in Iran—" I tried to protest.

"You could have ridden through a gun battle for all I care," Brynn tossed back. Her long blond hair was almost white as it shimmered in the sun. Her deep commanding voice boomed through the arena, making its way into my bones. "In here, you will do it my way. You will relearn. And then you will gallop in a safe way. Got it?"

I pulled Yakh to a halt, then slowly asked him to walk on. And walk we did. In meditative circles for weeks on end. Rather than be frustrated by my confinement to an arena, I decided to take the opportunity to really work on my craft. To get connected with my horse. To relearn how my body and his could fuse. To take the circles as patterns that would allow my mind to focus exclusively on Yakh and the lessons he had for me.

After many more months, I was ready for the speed I yearned for. Brynn had taught me to work with my horse's energy, to pull the energy inside me and channel it slowly. It wasn't about dominating the horse, she told me, but rather earning his respect. To do that, however, I would have to learn to trust and respect myself—a more difficult challenge.

When Yakh tried to buck me, I would grip with my entire body, afraid of falling in front of Brynn and the other women riders at the barn. If I fell, I would be disappointing my entire lineage.

But the riding and the delving back into Iran through my family, my notes, and the research I had kept locked away for years were bringing me back to life, reawakening my curiosity for the world around me. My lessons with Brynn and Yakh were teaching me to harness energy and strength. This in turn allowed me to find energy and balance in other areas of my life as well. I was learning patience, with myself, with my children, with my work. I was learning to accelerate and then downshift my speed on horseback and in life. I started to understand that I could harness the seemingly endless amount of energy that my kids exuded rather than be intimidated or exhausted by it. I started seeing them differently: as complex human beings vibrating with thought and inspiration. And I realized I could guide them to find their right speeds.

The lessons applied to my failed marriages too. My first marriage ended because I could not find the passion in surrendering to love. I felt a sense of paralysis, disorientation, and disconnection.

My second marriage was the opposite. I wanted to dominate him, wanted to make up for all that had gone wrong in my life—arrest and exile from my native home, a divorce, and giving birth to and parenting a baby as a single mother—through my attempt to control Peter. I wanted to mold him into my parents' ideas of the perfect partner. We bought a home with a fruit orchard and a pool in the backyard, and I thought I had finally arrived. But Peter didn't want to be dominated any more than I had. So he bucked. He pushed back on me when I told him we needed to buy more things, to take more expensive trips, to define our success based on the values of my Iranian-American community in Southern California, which were largely about excess. Peter wanted nothing to do with this lifestyle. So we fought. The more he bucked, the tighter I squeezed, not yet having internalized the reality that love is about finding the joy in surrender rather than trying to dominate your partner. After eight years together, in the midst of the viral pandemic of COVID-19, Peter and I filed for divorce.

In September 2021, on the anniversary of 9/11, I climbed up on Yakh. It was hard to believe it had been twenty years since I'd watched the towers fall from my tiny Manhattan apartment, with no idea what might come next. In the two decades since, I had lived a dozen lifetimes. Now, I was riding my way back into the loves that had ignited me during the first decade of the 2000s, trying to find my path. As I began looking up, thawing out, and starting to feel again, the world around me was spinning at an alarmingly high pace. Only a few days before, we had learned the Taliban had taken Kabul. I knew it was likely that soon they would also take Herat, where my friends and their horses were. The Taliban were also dangerously close to Mashad, where my remaining family in Iran lived.

Now, cantering around the arena on that September 11, my thoughts already a world away, Brynn came running, shouting that Herat had fallen, too.

"No! No, no, no, that can't be! That is just f—"

I didn't have a chance to complete the profanity. Yakh sensed the quickening of my heartbeat. As soon as I started yelling, he pinned his ears back, rolled his eyes into the back of his head, reared up, and bucked me off. In my shock, I didn't let go of the long leather reins, and they chafed the skin on my palms as Yakh dragged me around the arena. All of the other women riding or walking their horses stopped to look at me. My face flushed, burning my cheeks from the inside out. I had put all of my effort and energy into ensuring that I didn't fall. Instead of sliding into the joy of riding and letting go as I had done in Iran in the early 2000s, this time around my entire body habitually gripped the saddle in a war of wits between my horse and me.

I had fallen so many times in Iran, and that had nearly broken me. Then came the big fall on the beach in Santa Barbara. I was determined to forget about horses, erase the quickening of my pulse that only came with equine adrenaline filling my bones as I went careening through the hills of Iran. I had fallen in so many ways that I had locked Iran and horses, my greatest loves, away. But a chance discovery of the history of horses in my family, as well as the siren call of my homeland, brought them back to me in my forties. I realized I had been resisting riding because I did not want to fall. And after that fall by the sea, I was determined that no one should ever see me fall again. Falling was weakness. I could not afford weakness. But now, for the world to see as I pondered the fate of the world, I had fallen again, spectacularly.

I inhaled dirt, dust, and the particles of shit that created the footing of the arena. I turned my head toward the ground, willing it to open up and swallow me alive. Instead, my body began fusing with the earth, dirt covering every pore. Yakh continued dragging me for what felt like hours but was probably less than a minute.

"Let go!" I heard Brynn and several others shout. I shook my head and clenched my jaw, causing the sand to work its way between my teeth.

I. Will. Not. Let. Go.

It was bad enough that I had fallen, embarrassed myself, and betrayed my lineage. But then I thought about my grandmother and my aunts, imagining the Iranian horsewomen warriors whose blood coursed through my veins. Was falling failure or something else? Suddenly, I jackknifed my body so I could use my legs to slow us down. After years of internal struggle, of fighting with myself about where I belonged in the world, of raging against an ancestral homeland that disappointed me, of breaking one marriage and then another, I had been spiraling down into a depression that was deepened by self-pity. But in that moment something finally clicked: I could choose to focus on intergenerational trauma and my own pain, or I could be curious and learn from the intergenerational strength my grandmother and aunts had passed down to me.

"Halt, Yakh," I said in the calmest voice I could muster. He stopped. I stood up, brushed the dirt from my battered body, and looped my arms around his neck. "I'm going to let go now."

Everything fell into place as I dropped the reins to the ground and stood facing my horse. Instead of concentrating on Yakh, I had been immersed in thoughts about myself and the world. Even when I mounted him, I wasn't focused on him, his energy, and the pace he needed. He had been trying to show me that he needed to walk today, not trot or canter. That this day was a day of patience and reflection. That I could spend my time with my thoughts, but I had to slow my body and his in order to do so. Cadence. Rhythm. Patience. Why hadn't I understood?

I had done so well for so long. After years of riding and falling in Iran, then a decade of starving myself of the pleasure of horses, I had gotten back on a horse for an entire four years without falling. Each day, when my eyes begged my body to go back to sleep before the sunrise, I told myself that I had to ride because I was rewriting history. I would never fall again. And that determination forced me out of bed, day after day.

But something felt off every time I climbed up on Yakh's withers. That is, until the day I fell, demonstrating my failure for everyone to see. When I jackknifed my body, refusing to let go of the reins despite being dragged around the arena like cattle, something happened. I stood up and looked around. So long as I was afraid of falling, I wouldn't be able to respect or trust myself. As long as I lived in fear, I could never surrender to the joy of wonder and curiosity.

I had always thought that a fall like that would be world-ending. I expected the other women, Brynn included, to be laughing at me. My impostor syndrome was swallowing me. Everyone watched the fall. Now everyone knew I wasn't a "real" horse girl. I had let down my grandmother, who was surely looking down at me from somewhere in the universe.

But no one laughed. Instead, they rushed toward me, mouths agape. Brynn pulled me into an embrace, the one and only time she ever let her emotions show.

"You're a real cowgirl, you know that?" Brynn said. I was stunned into silence.

"I would have never survived a fall like that," one of the women said to me. "I would have been trampled. But you . . . look at you. I don't even know how you're standing in front of me."

"I fell," I said, still in shock.

"But it was spectacular," another woman said. "The best I've ever seen."

I looked at the seven pairs of female eyes transfixed on me. Brynn pulled back to survey me from head to toe.

"Pardis, I always knew you were a good rider, but I think you never realized how good a rider you truly are until today."

And then Ahu's words finally penetrated my soul: to ride is to fall. And rather than fixate on my falls and failures, I could concentrate on how many falls I had survived and how I had survived them. How each fall made me better. Stronger. I could finally ride free. Free of fear. I could surrender.

Ride Free

CLICK, CLACK, CRACKLE, CLACK. Click, clack, crackle, clack. The rhythmic beat of hooves was the perfect soundtrack for my new life up north, a life I had ridden into after my perfectly spectacular fall.

The day I stood up after being dragged around the arena in Scottsdale, Arizona, marked perhaps the most important turning point in my life to date. I understood the true soul-lightening pleasure of surrender as a way of life. To live is to ride. To ride is to fall. To live is to fall, and so in order to live one must not be afraid of falling. And once I embraced that, everything started falling into place.

The year 2021 was a difficult one: a divorce followed by living with three children amid a pandemic while trying to work full-time, parent full-time, and continue my riding. But I realized that the real weight I carried was the twin burdens of pride and fear. I had used pride and fear as defense mechanisms for a world that I found dangerous. One where I couldn't find my footing, didn't know where I belonged. But now I was recalibrating. Letting go. Surrendering. And the more I rode, the more I thawed out, opened up, looked up.

As I got back on my horses, opened myself back up to my heritage and lineage, discovered that horses were in my blood and were a way of carrying my culture with me, I realized that I needed to pause and reflect on the balance—or imbalance—of my life. I also realized that while I thought I had been walking through my professional life, sailing at times, I had actually been speed-racing through life, pounding forward at an unhealthy pace. I kept taking on more and more responsibility at work, seeking to rise, to ride harder and faster, to prove to everyone around me that not only could I ride but I wouldn't fall. And that fear of falling kept me on a tightrope. I had no clue I'd already lost my balance.

Arizona State University (ASU), where I was working as a dean by 2021, is America's most innovative university. And while it is a terrifically inspiring school, it challenged me as a leader. The competitive atmosphere and pace are grinding. Now couple that with living in the overheated, concrete jungle of a city whose infrastructure has not caught up to its growing population. I raced to work and spent my days running so fast that every meeting and every email blurred into the next. Then I spent hours driving my children through traffic to various indoor activities, trying to avoid the heat but also keep their bodies moving. At the end of the day, I would collapse—and often cry—in a heap of exhaustion. It was pure adrenaline, induced by a fear of failing or falling, that got me out of bed each morning.

When the pandemic hit, the exhaustion amplified to a point where there was no higher shot of adrenaline that could keep up. Now I was working from home while trying to care not only for my children but for thousands of students all at once. I was barely sleeping or eating. With each passing day of quarantine, it also became harder and harder for my ex-husband and me to ignore the reality that we could not stay living together, that the notion of conscious uncoupling couldn't work for us. We stayed in the trenches, hunkered down with one another through as much of the pandemic as possible. We coped. Neither of us enjoyed the other's company anymore, each a mirror to the other of our mutual faults and flaws.

But when I fell, and then got up, on that fall day in 2021, everything stood still. I realized I could fall and still stand. That falling meant I had been riding hard, that falling was a part of life, was *supposed* to happen.

I returned home that day and decided three things: (1) Peter and I needed to move out of our home and into separate spaces, (2) I needed to leave ASU and find a new job, and 3) my life was out of balance. Riding, and the lessons I was learning from my horse, guided me forward. I realized that the attention I paid to the rhythms of Yakh's hoofbeats, the energy of his that I harnessed and channeled, and the patience with which I had to approach working with an animal who outweighed me by at least ten times were all the roadmap for life I needed. And the balance of learning when to speed up, slow down, walk, trot, or canter applied to *everything*.

Within three months Peter and I sold our house and moved to separate apartments, and then I found a new job in a dream location. The University of Montana was looking for a provost, a leader who could be innovative and authentic at the same time. I had been dreaming of riding through the mountains and rivers of Montana for years.

The first time I visited Missoula, something stirred in my heart. Snow-capped peaks kissed soaring big skies. Rivers tumbled into lush banks surrounded by pine trees. I saw horses at every turn. But what spoke to me most, what gave my soul the peace I had been longing for at last, was the pace. No one rushed to work or pounded through their day. People took time to appreciate their surroundings, to live in harmony with the earth, to embody a reverence for balance in life. Balance. Surrender. Live.

But moving wasn't going to be easy. Peter refused to join me in Montana, preventing me from taking our sons out of state. Tara, my eleven-year-old daughter from my first marriage, and I would move north alone to try to reinvent ourselves and make a new life. And, just as my ex-husband did not want my boys to leave Phoenix for Montana, Brynn didn't want Yakh leaving the barn in Scottsdale. So Tara and I decided to buy ourselves two horses for our new life in Missoula. This time, I decided, I would buy the horse of my dreams.

Riding a Quarter Horse around an arena had been fun and taught me a great deal. But I knew myself well enough to know that what drew me to riding in the first place was the siren call of nature. The first time my heart had stirred for horses was standing in the middle of a field surrounded by mountains outside of Tehran. Now I was moving to the mountains and could ride the hills to my heart's content. I didn't want to be a rider who forced my horse to ride in circles or jump over gates and stones. Though I respected my hunter/jumper English-riding friends in Arizona, I wanted the freedom of riding for hours and miles on end, reconnecting with the earth and sky above. I refused to force myself into a hole that I didn't fit. I wasn't going to settle for stumbling into situations any longer. I wanted to trail-ride, and I needed to find the horse who could help me do so safely. It wasn't about showing or eventing. It was not about jumping over a hurdle or racing around a barrel. I wanted to be safe. I wanted to be in nature. I was finally not afraid of surrender—had, in fact, found the joy and hope that surrender brings. And I wanted to be with a horse who could continue to teach me as much as I taught him.

While there are hundreds of horse breeds throughout the world, the breeds divide into two main groups as far as movement is concerned: gaited and non-gaited horses. The primary difference between the two is in the movement of the horse's legs, which is felt most precisely by the mounted rider. Gaited horses are usually smoother to ride than non-gaited horses, owing to what is referred to as their "footfall," or the way they place their legs. A gaited horse will walk similarly to human beings by placing one foot in front of the other. When they speed up, they simply increase this diagonal stride, moving a front foot and the opposite rear foot simultaneously. There is always one foot on the ground at any given time to support the rider.

A non-gaited horse, however, moves its two front legs in opposition to its two back legs in more of a hopping motion. This is particularly felt at higher speeds, where the trot or canter is more jarring to the rider owing to the leg position of the horse. This jarring effect is felt by the rider of a non-gaited horse because of the freefall experienced by the horse and rider on the down beat—the rise and then fall needed by the horse to take one step of the trot to the next step. A gaited horse is better for covering a lot of terrain and longer rides because of its smoothness. A non-gaited horse is best suited to short bursts of energy—i.e., for races—or for cow herding.

Most of the horses in the United States are not gaited, while most of the horses in places like Iran and Iceland are gaited. This, according to horse scholars, is because horses considered "primitive breeds," or breeds that have been around for more than five thousand years, are mostly gaited horses. The oldest horse breeds on the planet today are Icelandic, Fjord, Akhal-Teke, Mongolian, Arabian, and Caspian. These breeds are all (or were all at one time) gaited horses, which is what was needed during the time of empires 5,400 years ago: horses that could cover miles and miles of terrain in a day while carrying their rider smoothly so that armies, for instance, could fight atop their horses. Over time, Arabian horses, popular for showing and racing, lost their "gait," their ability to move their legs in opposition.

In the United States, several gaited breeds, thought to have descended mostly from Caspian, Mongolian, and Turkoman horses, still exist. The three most popular breeds, named for their American geographies, are Tennessee Walkers, Missouri Fox Trotters, and Mountain Pleasure Horses. These horses are still used by Americans who wish to trail ride, covering long distances on a smoother jaunt.

The more I learned about the rich history of horses and how they had evolved on different continents, the more enchanted I became. I watched videos of Caspian horses and Missouri Fox Trotters side by side with Quarter Horses and observed the difference in movement between a gaited and non-gaited horse.

I read about gaited horse breeds in the United States, looking closely at the difference in the horses' bodies, and read everything I could about their personalities.

I knew I needed a gaited horse. The difference between the three most popular gaited horses, as far as I could tell, was their size and generalized temperament. Tennessee Walkers are the largest of the group, standing at fifteen hands tall and weighing in at over 1,500 pounds. Mountain Pleasure Horses, on the other hand, were rumored as the most stubborn of the gaited breeds but also the most dependable. Missouri Fox Trotters—known for their smaller size, their gentle curiosity, and their rocking, gliding trot that make the rider feel as if they were fox-trotting across a dance floor—spoke to me most. This was only confirmed when I sat on my first Missouri Fox Trotter. The horse's body moved exactly like the horses I had ridden in Iran. Its torso was also more oval compared to the boxy Quarter Horse I had been riding. And its strides were long but smooth, not choppy, not bouncy. I was in love.

In preparation for our move to Montana in the winter of 2022, Tara and I first flew to Missouri to meet a breeder and a trainer whose work together reportedly produced Missouri Fox Trotters that were among the best horses in the world. Dave and Trent are a truly formidable pair. Dave finds the best horses to breed. And Trent, a former killer whale trainer for Sea World, embodies the same behavioralist philosophies in horsemanship that I had witnessed in Iran. The moment I walked onto their farm, I knew our fates were sealed.

En route to St. Louis, I had also received word from Doug Antczak, an equine genealogist at Cornell University who has been studying the lineage of primitive horse breeds, including

the Caspian horse, for decades. His most recent research revealed a possible genetic connection between Caspian horses and Missouri Fox Trotters in particular.

The first time I laid eyes on the palomino blonde Fox Trotter who would prove to be my soulmate, I knew Doug was right. Like Caspian horses, Missouri Fox Trotters are smaller in stature but feature pronounced necks and full jawlines. Their chests are as expansive as their hips—like Caspians and Akhal-Tekes—in strong contrast to the American Quarter Horse, whose hind ends are significantly larger. And riding them confirmed the connection. Like Caspians, the Fox Trotters have shorter legs that are deceptive; their strides are long because they don't just move their legs but initiate the movement from their shoulders. When Dave told me that the stallion who sired the two brothers Tara and I wanted was possibly part Caspian, I was sold.

The palomino was the stronger, feistier of the two, so he became my horse. I named him Caspian. The first time I called out his nickname, "Cas," he nodded his head and tossed his mane as he proudly trotted around the arena. His brother was not blond but rather chocolate brown with a perfect white stripe down his nose. His hair shaded from brown to red, changing in the sunlight.

"He is just beautiful," Tara marveled as she watched him gallop around Dave and Trent's farm. "I think I'll name him J.B."

"J.B.? Like Joe Biden?" I asked my daughter. She laughed, tossed her long macaroni curls, and shook her head.

"Not Joe Biden, Mom. Just Beautiful."

The move to Montana was the start of a new phase of my life, one marked by balance, peace, and an all-encompassing beauty. I bookend my days and weeks with activities that bring me joy. It is a joy that I can only truly feel in my practice because I have learned to surrender to myself and my horse, to surrender to the world around me rather than try to live in the grips of fear. Each morning I rise with the chickens I inherited with the purchase of our new home. I greet the sun with them and then write for an hour or more. Then I go to work at the University of Montana, where my new colleagues brim with ideas and I have the great fortune of working with and channeling that energy. As soon as the clock tower bells announce that it's 5 p.m., I rush out of the office and drive to the barn to see Caspian. The long summer Montana days, where the sun does not set until 10 or 11 p.m., make it possible to spend hours riding into the sunset. I ride every night out into the hills and through the rivers, relishing every moment with Caspian as we are enveloped in a blanket of green and blue beauty on the trails.

That life-changing fall in Arizona woke me up in more ways than one. It allowed me to face my fears and realize that I could fall and be curious about my fall, and its effect on me, and then focus on my strength in getting up and back on the horse. That surrender meant I could truly live, moving with vulnerability and curiosity. I didn't need to fear falling anymore. Because when I did fall, no one laughed or judged me, least of all myself. Hitting the ground gave me a new perspective. It allowed me to stop, pause, think, diagnose my surroundings. Falling may have been a type of failure, but some failures are necessary in life to help us see what we can truly become.

When I hit the ground that day and then stood up, I realized I could let myself fall from a failing marriage and an unfulfilling career. Those moments of free fall, which were many long months in my personal and professional life, were indeed terrifying. But I had the solace of knowing that while I'd take a hit, the earth would support me, and I'd get back up and be a better rider, a better mother, leader, feminist, writer. And that is exactly what happened.

Extricating myself from Arizona, ASU, and my marriage were the moments of free fall. I hit the ground, left ASU, and got divorced. Leaving Arizona to move to Montana was not without lasting injury. I had to leave my boys behind with their father, a stab that left a deep-purple bruise on my heart that will never heal. But like my other scars and bruises, I learn to live *with* them and appreciate them—just as I appreciate the bruises Caspian gives me when he bumps me, when he is sending me a signal I need to heed.

With the help of my trainer, Trent, as well as Caspian's never-ending trove of patience, I understand that fear is what has been bubbling inside me for the past twenty years. And that fear has been eating away at me and prohibiting me from fully feeling the joy of my practice. To ride is to fall. To fall and get back up is to find strength in freedom and surrender.

Riding is pure joy pouring into my soul and out of my body into the world around me. The lessons I learn from my practice have a ripple effect throughout my life.

Trent and Caspian teach me about clear, confident communication. Harnessing Caspian's energy by absorbing some inside me and then mirroring that back to him brings balance and harmony to us both. Clear communication that sets up my expectations and allows me to listen keeps us both safe. It is the same in my leadership role. I harness my colleagues' energy, shape it, and bring it back to them with a vision and roadmap for change. And like with Caspian, communicating to my faculty and staff clearly with a strong message of change-inspired confidence brings them along in a positive way because I am also listening to them.

"A horse needs a clear leader. Someone who is consistent, confident, and unwavering in giving him direction," Trent reminds me. "He needs that to survive and thrive. He needs you to be gentle and loving, yes, but firm with boundaries. He needs to trust you."

That's leadership.

On the occasional days when Caspian misbehaves, biting me or trotting off before I have both feet in stirrups, I realize that I haven't approached him with the right energy—and that's on me, not him. As such, I am the one who needs more practice. I am distracted by something else, immersed as I am in our culture of multitasking. But I can't do that with my horse, any more than I can do that with my children. I have to give them my full attention. Be patient, calm, and loving, but firm with boundaries. When my boys visit me, I drop everything else and focus only on them. And when Tara and I are together at home, I need to listen deeply to her and bring her energy and mine into balance.

Riding—and falling—have shaped and transformed my life for decades. But it took a bad fall and a move to Montana to help me understand that this practice is my life, and it is just that: a lifelong practice. One that makes me better in every way.

"Desensitize your horse to the thing that scares him most," Trent tells me, an echo of Ahu's words that had reverberated in my bones. "Do it over and over again until it isn't scary. Be there to love him through the things that terrify him. And make them peaceful for him until he is at peace, too."

As I work to desensitize Caspian to loud noises, the sight of a training stick, or the fear of entering a trailer, I learn to face my own fears. I begin writing with a fervor again, facing my fears of failing and writing from a place of surrender. Like my horse, I can give in to the thing that scares me most—failing.

And once I accept it as one of several possibilities, I find the freedom to sort through my thoughts and get words on paper.

The more I ride Caspian, challenging him to new sights and sounds, the more comfortable I become not just in my own body but with my own thoughts. I spent a decade pushing thoughts from my mind. Thoughts of my expulsion from Iran, of not one but two failed marriages, of the violence I experienced at the hands of certain men throughout my life. Now I welcome the frightening thoughts. I realize that what I have lived through is indeed trauma, and while I can focus on the pain, I can also focus on the strength that saw me through these falls and got me up again. The moment of hitting the ground is always scary, but the moment of standing and getting back on the horse is triumphant.

I have also finally started leading in the way I wanted to lead when I first became a department chair and then a dean. By leaning into the bold change I believe higher education needs to engage, rather than running from or dancing around structural change, I take it on headfirst. In understanding my role as a leader, as with my horse, I commit to a direction and then earn trust by following through.

At home, I tell my kids about my terrors and help Tara and my boys face theirs: Finding comfort in the dark. Watching a thunderstorm to see the beauty of lightning illuminating the sky rather than hiding under the sheets. Telling a friend how much they have hurt our feelings and seeing the relief in their faces when honest emotions flow through. We face our fears over and over again until we find peace.

And that peace comes to me daily, every time I ride.

I started out riding alone after work. As I drove into the barn and began sorting through the brushes I wanted to use and the riding equipment that seemed right for the day, I'd take slow, deep breaths, reminding myself to slow down to absorb this practice and its benefits fully. It occurred to me that while I have been riding for nearly two decades, it wasn't until I moved to Montana that I took the time to reflect on the intricate details of my hobby and how they have sutured with the other aspects of my life. The big skies, the perfect beat of a gaited horse's strides, and a trainer who knows the same stories as my people in Iran have given me the space I needed.

Slowing my practice down, I take the time to communicate with my horse the way my ancestors did. I make hand motions in front of Caspian before mounting him so that he is attuned to me. I bow to him and nod my chin to get him to stop. And once he is locked in on me, then I mount him. I ride in the arena for hours at a time without losing my patience or getting bored because now I fully appreciate every subtle movement that Caspian and I make together. We build a foundation of trust and respect so that when I do fall, I do so safely.

It began as a daily practice alone, just Caspian and me, but now, three or four times a week, I join a group of women from my barn to hit the trails. While I learned to trail ride in a group in Iran and had loved herd riding, when I started riding in the United States I preferred to go it alone. I was afraid of others seeing my failures and my falls. But in Missoula, Montana, I have found a group of women who support me as much as my Iranian sisters. When I fail, they praise me for recognizing and correcting my mistakes. And they help me find my feet out there on the unpredictable trail.

After the incident at the beach, I had mostly stopped riding outside of an arena. The terror of unknown variables in nature, a fear of getting lost, and a lack of confidence kept me from my greatest joy—trail riding. At the barn in Arizona, no one wanted to trail ride. They were focused almost fully on jumping their horses and fancy tricks in the arena. I tried to fit in with this approach, but arena riding, while inspiring because I got to be back on a horse and working on my craft, didn't give me the same high as hitting the open trail.

In Missoula, everyone I meet wants to trail ride. And I have the perfect horse for covering miles of mountain terrain. When I initially announced to friends and family that I was moving to Montana, they all looked at me quizzically. What was I, a city girl who was raised in Southern California, lived in New York City, and studied in Tehran, going to do in such a rural context? Most of them had never visited the Treasure State, turned off by its remote location and inaccessibility.

"So, you're heading to the North then?" my brother had asked. He and I are big fans of the *Game of Thrones* (*GOT*) books and television series. His reference to the "North" was a *GOT* term, describing one of the many lands in the fictional world created by author George R. R. Martin. Much of the action in the series takes place in the warmer southern lands or the worlds near bodies of water. From my perspective, and that of many other *GOT* fans, the North, while harsh, cold, and remote, carried a certain reverence. This is why the main protagonist, Jon Snow, travels ever farther toward the North throughout the series and in his own personal journey. And it is his time in the farthest northern reaches, what is referred to as "north of the Wall," that permits him the space to reflect, heal, find peace, and make decisions about his future.

"This is the season of my life where I'll be north of the Wall," I told my brother.

Though Montana is known for its long, harsh winters, I arrived just as the spring showers were giving way to summer. I moved to Missoula on June 1, 2022, with my daughter, Tara, my dog, Bella, and our two horses. As we drove into town, the most spectacular shades of forest green greeted us. Rounded green hills rolled into cresting, jagged peaks dotted with pine, aspen, and fir trees. Tall, lush grass guided us to rambling rivers that wound their way through town and into the mountains. My heart lifted as this fairy-tale setting enveloped us, welcoming us home.

Within days, I had settled Caspian at my new barn, owned by a lovely Montanan couple who own several gaited horses themselves. After watching me work alone with Caspian in the arena for a few days, Anna, the barn owner, invited me to join her and another friend for a trail ride. I could hardly contain my excitement. I readied my horse for the first of many trail rides that would soothe my soul.

Anna, Sara, and I mounted our horses, and we were off. As soon as we were outside of the barn gates, Caspian licked his lips to indicate his joy. He tossed his head and picked his feet up off the ground, proudly ensuring me a smooth ride. It was as though he wanted to show the other two horses how much we fit in.

He sped up to keep pace with the others, and I felt the exhilaration of flying once again—careening through the grass, up and down the twists and turns.

"I. Am. Flying!" I shouted as we rode through a river, the cool water splashing around my legs.

Perfect whispers of warm wind blew into my hair, kissing my forehead and Caspian's mane. The leaves shimmered an almost golden green as the wind gently wound through them. Caspian carried me toward the heart-quickening sound of the river. As we rode along the riverbank, the last of the day's sunlight dappling in between the trees and casting pebble-like shadows onto the water, I felt tears flowing from my eyes down my cheeks, into my mouth. They were tears of absolute joy. I was grateful to taste the salty water, a reminder that this moment was indeed real.

As the sun began to set, igniting the big sky a hundred shades of pink and orange, we rode into the hills, cresting the top just in time to see the golden glow of the mountains that surrounded us. We had ridden through a lavender field on our ascent, and Caspian was still munching on some remainders; I caught the subtle scent of it combined with the intoxicating smell of horse hay and dirt that lived permanently in his fur.

Without the lows of failing and falling, I could never have appreciated the high of that moment. I have learned to surrender. This is a feeling that many hyphenated people who struggle with belonging never have the luxury of knowing because we live in a heightened state of danger and fear. Society tells us stories about ourselves we don't recognize, so we keep fighting, pushing, using the fear of falling to drive us away from the weightlessness of surrender. But now I know it doesn't matter if I fall again. I know I will stand and ride again and again and again. I looked at my surroundings, my eyes drinking in the hues of gold, pink, and orange of the sky as it wrapped around the green landscape. I listened to the whispers of the wind, the roar of the river now in the distance, as Caspian neighed his approval. I closed my eyes and inhaled peace. This was the ride of my life.